PROMISES, PROMISES, PROMISES

Promises, Promises, Promises

Joel Nederhood

Board of Publications
of the Christian Reformed Church

© 1979 by the Board of Publications
   of the Christian Reformed Church
   2850 Kalamazoo SE
   Grand Rapids, MI 49560

Library of Congress Cataloging in Publication Data

Nederhood, Joel H
     Promises, promises, promises.

     SUMMARY: Discusses God's promises to Christians
which are revealed in the Bible.
     1. God—Promises—Meditation. [1.   God—
Promises. 2.   Christian life] I.   Title.
BT180.P7N43   231'.7   79-18889
ISBN 0-933140-09-6

Contents

Foreword

Over the last two thousand years libraries have been written about the Bible. This is another book about that book.

Promises, Promises, Promises is compact, direct, and personal. Written for the Christian who's becoming mature, this book doesn't intend to rival scholarly essays or lengthy commentaries. It's meant as a confession, a collection of twenty-eight candid reflections written by a Christian who has lived intimately with Scripture for nearly five decades.

Although this book is likely to receive a wider reading, it was originally planned as part of a young adult course published by the Christian Reformed Church's Education Department. The title of that course is *Voices*, and it provides an in-depth study of the Scriptures. Both that course and this book were published at a time when the Bible was being greatly debated. It's meant, of course, to be greatly believed. This book was written to aid faith, not fuel another fiery debate.

The title, *Promises, Promises, Promises*, works two ways. In a world decorated with slick advertising, campaign pledges, and broken romances, it's easy to turn cynical and to dourly conclude that life is nothing but unkept promises, promises, promises....

Even the most casual reader of the Bible soon discovers that those pages are also smothered with promises, the ones that are kept by God. If we read the Bible seriously, we must contend with those promises: Either God tells the truth, and we have to believe it, or we should indict Him for perjury on the evidence of this book. There is no other alternative. The Bible is a record of promises, promises, and more promises. The reader's only choice is whether or not to believe them.

The author of this book is Joel Nederhood, Director and Minister of the Back to God Hour, an international broadcasting ministry of the Christian Reformed Church. Dr. Nederhood is a graduate of Calvin College and Calvin Seminary (Grand Rapids, Michigan) and of the Free University (Amsterdam).

The author and the editors hope that those who read the chapters of *Promises, Promises, Promises* will also read passages of Scripture listed at the close of each chapter. All you're reading now is our book. It would be a shame if you passed by an opportunity to read God's.

A. JAMES HEYNEN
DIRECTOR OF EDUCATION

CHAPTER ONE

Promises, Promises, Promises

"Ouch—Frithrah!" Oh, pardon me. I shouldn't begin a book about the Bible with a swear word.

Perhaps you're saying, "Don't worry. If it's a swear word, most people will never know." If you recognized the word, you're probably saying, "You can use *Frithrah* if you want to. Even though it's a swear word, it's not a regular swear word. It's a swear word only rabbits use. So go ahead—people won't mind and rabbits won't read your book."

Maybe by now you're beginning to think this whole discussion is ridiculous. You may be one of those people who thinks rabbits don't talk. Well, they do talk. What's more, I know what they say. In fact, a lot of people know what rabbits say—everyone who's read Richard Adam's book *Watership Down.*

Watership Down is a remarkable book that literally takes you into another world, the world of rabbits. As you read the book, you feel like you've become part of the rabbit culture. Bunnies with nervous noses become real-life characters with colorful personalities. You enter a rabbit world where the sun is named *Frithrah.* Since the sun is also their god, rabbits take the sun's name in vain, using *Frithrah!* as profanity. In this world a motor is a *hrududu,* a luncheon date is a *silflay,* and *hraka* is something no rabbit with any sense of decency would ever drop inside his home. It's a world in which rabbits show courage, fear, and cunning, and live in the expectation that they will one day be carried into immortality by the great Silver Rabbit.

1

Some people think that reading the Bible is like reading *Watership Down*, that both books take us into another world. And in a sense the Bible does remove us from our ordinary setting. It lifts us above our daily routine, giving us an incredible, panoramic view. We look back to the dawn of creation and, turning, to the end of time. We get a new perspective, a wholly different way of looking at life. In that sense, the Bible *does* lift us out of this world to a new reality all its own.

But the differences between the two books are even more striking. In *Watership Down* I was introduced to the rabbits' world so intensely I'll never again see one of those critters without wondering about its family, health, and name. But in the Bible I'm introduced with even greater intensity to the *real* world; I now see everything around me differently: The whimpering child, boiling volcano, and peacefully dying grandmother—all look different now. In *Watership Down* we see an unreal world creatively made by an author; in the Bible we meet the Author of the real world, and it is *we* who are creatively remade. *Watership Down* shows us Frithrah, the sun, the light of the rabbits' lives; the Bible shows us Jesus, the Son, the Light of the world by whom we see, or without whom we are blind.

Watership Down, you see, like any good novel, pulls us out of the world. But the Bible, like no other book, acquaints us with this world. In fact, from the smell of bacon in the morning to the glow of a spectacular sunset, we do not really know this world until we have immersed ourselves in God's Word. It's not enough to take hold of the Bible once in a while, reading a verse here or a passage there. We must let the Bible take hold of us, completely, "no holds barred." Then, and only then, will we genuinely know the world, and our calling, and our future.

Some people, of course, may see too much of the world. By the time they're young adults, they're cynical about all of life. Fathers promised them evenings at home, but when evening came, fathers were gone. Mothers promised they'd always be there, but even mothers die. And through it all, advertisers claim that booze can get you pleasure, cars can fetch you status, and everyone lives happily ever after in a split-level home with a pool. You don't have to be very old to notice that life looks very much like a wilderness strewn with promises, promises, promises . . . .

2

But now go to the Bible for an antidote to cynicism. Here you'll discover that in the middle of the landscape littered with broken promises there is a cross badly stained with very human blood. On that cross a promise first made in Eden was finally kept. And if you look behind the cross, you'll see an empty tomb. When the corpse they had installed in that tomb marched out on Easter morning, King of kings and Lord of lords, every promise made by God was made sure. The Bible offers a perspective which can replace all the broken promises.

Over the years most of us have been taught that there are many (66) books in the Bible. But in a more important way, the Bible is—from Genesis to Revelation—a single book. And this single book has one major theme: It's all about God's promised rescue of His people, His promised repair of all creation. Closely related to the single theme of redemption is the fact that the Bible is about one person: Jesus of Nazareth, the promised Redeemer. In John 5:39 Jesus insisted that even the Old Testament talks about Him. Not only chapters like Isaiah 53 or Psalm 22, which clearly speak of Jesus, but *all* of the Old Testament involves the promised Messiah. So the Bible is one book, with one theme and one main character. This unity is possible because ultimately the Bible has only one Author, God Himself. Even though many people had a hand in the writing, it is finally God who stands behind every sentence and every word. The Bible is the Word of God.

I'd like to suggest that you spend some time each week reading in the Gospels, Matthew, Mark, Luke, or John. One reason for this suggestion is that the Gospels remind us God has faithfully kept His promise of redemption and keeps His promises to us even when we are surrounded by broken promises everywhere else. But I also encourage this practice because the Gospels are, I feel, the center of the Bible. It's easy to sometimes bog down in difficult parts of Scripture and lose sight of the single theme or main character of this one book. The Gospels lift us out of those moments and give us perspective again.

Because God, through His Holy Spirit, wrote the Bible, reading the Bible is like reading no other book. The same Spirit who filled the pages of Scripture fills the lives of all God's children. So when a Spirit-filled person reads the Spirit-written book, a unique correspondence is set up. Something within us is in tune with something within the Bible, and that "something" is God's Spirit.

To read the Bible is one thing; to understand it, and then believe it, is something else. The Bible is understandable and believable only when we know something about God and His covenant.

Covenant—what does that mean? Well, if you take a look at the Bible you'll notice it's divided into two parts: the Old Testament and the New Testament. And a testament is a covenant. Simple? Sure.

What's a *testament*? Well, you've heard of a "last will and testament," haven't you? A testament is a promise. A covenant is a promise, or a set of promises. Here's an example: marriage. Sometimes marriage is called a covenant. "Do you, Mary, solemnly covenant (promise) to take John, here present, as your wedded husband?" And Mary says, "Yes." So Mary and John make a covenant together, and the preacher says, "I now pronounce you man and wife." Marriage is a covenant in which two people promise to love, honor, and be faithful to each other.

The Bible is a book about a God who *covenants* with His people—that is, He makes promises to them and asks promises in return. The most basic promise God makes is, "I will be your God." In return, He asks this promise of us: "We will be your people." If the promises are kept, there is a partnership between God and His people, both committed to redeeming the fallen creation.

What becomes clear when reading the Bible is that, in the covenant partnership between God and people, only God is faithful. The promises people make to God are no more likely to be kept than the promises people make to other people.

But the Word of God is different. What God promises, He delivers. He has promised to deliver all who seek Him. If we read the Bible looking for God, we are guaranteed to find Him.

Suggested Bible Readings
God made the world. He made it good—like a garden. So it's good for us to be here, in God's good creation. It's even better to

4

be here with Christ. His presence transforms even a wild mountaintop into a garden.

Genesis 1, 2; Psalms 8, 104; Luke 9:28-36

CHAPTER TWO

The Greatest Fact

We are usually plunged into the three opening chapters of Genesis without the slightest warning about what we're getting into, and that's a major misfortune. We're given the impression that these chapters are not all *that* much different from other interesting stories we read first as children.

But the opening chapters of the Bible are, in fact, in a class by themselves. Here we read the "birth announcement" of the universe; these chapters take us back to the very dawn of time when there was literally nothing but God. I can hardly make my mind even *think* about how far back in time these words take us. To have material like this in my Bible, between two ordinary covers, almost makes my skin crawl. It's eerie when you think about it.

These three chapters deal with events that are fundamental, absolutely basic to all that follows. As one scholar has noted (Alexander Heidel of the University of Chicago), the *differences* between the creation account we have in the Bible and, for example, the Babylonian story of creation are far more important than the *similarities*. Another scholar (Hendrick Van Leeuwen) has pointed out very clearly that Genesis 1, 2, and 3 are, as a matter of fact, designed to fight myths—they are anti-mythological. These chapters destroy all the false ways people have tried to explain the origin of the world, of humanity, and of the evil that plagues us. They destroy false religions. They give us the truth.

Yet these first three chapters of Genesis are so grand that they can't be discussed in ordinary language; they have an air of mystery about them.

It's possible for an engineer to describe in detail how he builds a bridge or an airplane, but if God told us in detail how He made the universe, we'd never understand. This material is even different from Bible passages where ordinary historical events are handled. The opening chapters of the Bible deal with *special* history and are written with a special air of mystery.

The mystery with which Genesis 1, 2, and 3 are written is not the kind of mystery we "solve." Take the days of creation, for example. People question whether the first days were twenty-four hours long since the heavenly bodies were not created until day four. Some Christian scientists suggest long periods of time for the days of creation; others hold steadfastly to twenty-four-hour days for all six creation days. I have my own feelings on this subject, but I have to admit that they are just that, *feelings.* I haven't settled this issue in my own mind. To me, what's important and startling about the creation account is that God connects what *He* did with what *we* do. Creation took *days* to accomplish—six of them. God worked six days and then entered into His rest. We work six days and enter into ours. And someday, when our lives are over, we will enter into His rest too (Heb. 4:1).

Or think about the creation of woman from Adam's rib—that puzzles me. As a boy I accepted that simply as a fact, and I've never seriously doubted that this is history. But it is *curious* history, with elements that seem peculiar and strange. What's important in this account, I think, is not *how* woman was created, but what we see in the relationship between man and woman. God is telling me here about the closeness of the sexes (maleness and femaleness are *not* absolute opposites), about our need of one another, and about sex and marriage. But Adam's rib...this *is* mysterious history.

I expect the elements of mystery in these first chapters of the Bible will continue to excite my curiosity in whatever years I have left. And I expect, too, the day will come when I'll see exactly what these chapters mean. When I do, I'll probably wonder why I didn't see it more clearly before. For now, what's most important in these chapters are not the questions they raise but the answers they offer. In these chapters we find information about God and about people that we can find nowhere else. Here's information about a very young world, a very stunning mercy. God and humanity, the world and mercy—we cannot think straight about any of these, or about the Bible itself, unless we have the data of Genesis 1, 2, and 3. It would be a serious mistake if I were to disregard the great truths these chapters contain simply because certain elements continue to mystify me.

The most obvious fact revealed in these chapters is also the most important: God is the Creator.

I sometimes wonder what it would be like to believe that billions of things, Arabs and Zambians, alligators and zebras, azaleas and zinnias evolved from a ball of cosmic space dust. Some people believe this. At least they say they do. How can they? But when I think about them, I hear myself say, "Look what *you* believe—you believe that God is the origin of everything. And who is God? You've never seen Him. He is just God. And you believe that He created everything out of *nothing*. Now how can anyone believe *that?*

Well, I believe this because I believe the Bible tells the truth about God's creative work. I'll never escape the fact that my faith is dependent on these first chapters of the Bible. The God who addresses me throughout the rest of the Bible, and the rest of my life, is the Creator of all.

I remember two weeks my wife and I spent in another family's house; we were caring for the children while their parents were away. Everything in the house—the clothing in the closets, the pipe and tobacco in the study, the arrangement of the furniture—constantly reminded us of the owners. In the same way the evidence of the Creator surrounds us in the world. Can you look at the Grand Canyon and not see the Creator? Can you hear a child's first words and not hear God? I can't. And it's the Bible that puts me in touch with this great Creator.

Knowing God is Creator of the universe also helps me react properly to the world I live in. Because of Genesis 1 and 2 I know that the creation itself is extremely important.

Several years ago it suddenly struck me that God is a materialist. It seemed almost blasphemous at first because I'd heard materialism condemned so often. Nevertheless, Genesis 1 certainly tells us that God is extremely interested in material things; in fact, we know God loves His creation. If it were not for God's deliberate creation of the universe, there wouldn't be any

8

beautiful universe. The Bible tells us that, as creation unfolded, God stepped back at the end of each day and declared that what He'd made was *very* good.

Materialism is bad for us when we make gods of material things. But if God is the origin of all the world around us and is interested in it, we may study it, and claim it, and marvel at it throughout our lives. I ought to remember this every three or four years when I have to paint my house. Frankly, I don't like the job; I'd much prefer reading a book or writing. But if I can remember that painting a house is as good as singing a hymn, because both can praise God for His good creation, I may enjoy the task a little more.

The first three chapters of Genesis give a foundation to my thinking about God and the universe. At the same time, strange as it may seem, they have become the foundation for my thinking about myself. What I've found in them has made me feel extremely important; the facts there have lifted me up, given me self-understanding and self-respect.

Many years ago I sat in the study of a wise missionary who was an expert on Indian mysticism. Contrasting the Christian view of man with the non-Christian, he said that non-Christian religions tend to reduce the importance of individual persons. He described festivals he had seen in the Orient in which large idols were taken out of the temple and carried through the street; the people lay flat in the road, with their mouths in the dust, as the idol went by. They wanted to be destroyed in the presence of the idol because their religion turned them into a zero. But Christianity, my friend said, lifts people; it exalts them.

The first chapters of Genesis tell me I'm an "image bearer" of God. My father, Adam, was God's son. All my fellow humans and I are something like God.

Now it's true that the information these chapters give us about humanity is not entirely encouraging. Part of the story told here is of the devastating event we know as the fall. Who can calculate the damage that horrendous event has caused? There is great mystery surrounding God's actions reported in the opening chapters of the Bible, but there is also great mystery surrounding Adam and Eve's behavior. How Adam a voluntarily turn from God to Satan is something r ever be able to understand. We must never fo

9

entered the universe because of human rebellion. I have to re-mind myself of this all the time because it is easy for me to blame God for sin, or cancer, or hell.

The opening chapters of the Bible give me information I need to understand myself. I'm an image bearer, but fallen. Later, the Bible tells me that because I belong to Christ through faith, I am a fallen image bearer whom God is continually repairing through His Holy Spirit. These ideas—image bearer, fallen, re-deemed—help explain why I am as I am.

Sometimes the fact that I'm fallen stuns me, and I don't think I'll ever be able to pick myself out of the dirt again. But the fact that God made me, and is helping me be more fully His child—that fact stuns me even more.

What finally grips me as I look again at the first three chapters of Genesis is that God mercifully redeemed not only me but His whole creation. Genesis 3 ends in a shambles, with the curses of God raining down on all of us, on men as men, on women as women, on the hapless serpent, and even on the earth itself. But right there, amid the ruins, I see Jesus. And I remember that His bruised heel crushed Satan's head at Calvary. I remember that it is Jesus who will destroy the destroyer, put death to death, and restore life to the children of Adam and Eve. I see the mercy of the Lord sweeping over the smoldering battlefield where our father Adam lost to Satan. I see Jesus, already dressed in the wounds of battle, planting the banner of God's victory. And I know that His victory is our victory too.

In these opening chapters of the Bible I've found the truth on which I can build my life. Take that truth away, and that will be the end of me.

Suggested Bible Readings
During the first centuries of human history, Satan's seed sprouts first and fastest. It threatens to choke out the woman's seed. But God doesn't let that happen. He clears the field and starts a new planting. This time the two seeds will grow together until the time of harvest.

Genesis 4, 5, 6, 7, 8, 9; Matthew 13:24-30

CHAPTER THREE

The Beginning of Now

Kool-Aid laced with cyanide and Mr. John Wayne Gacey—two symbols representing the ugliness of our time. The Kool-Aid was gulped in the jungles of Guyana by the wretched followers of Rev. James Jones, the man who wanted to be God. And Mr. Gacey, carpenter, contractor, sometimes clown, murdered more than thirty young men; he threw a few bodies into a nearby river and buried the rest under and around his house. Mr. Gacey's suburban home is not far from mine.

None of us can deny that a wretched quality of evil is part of our time. It seems to be a part of human life...as much a part as eating is. This evil has been steaming along for centuries. Sometimes it erupts in the mass killing of a whole race—as it did in Nazi Germany—or earlier, when the Turks did away with a million-and-a-half Armenians in the 1920s.

But if the evil that lies like a deadly blanket over everything upsets us, what is more upsetting is that evil doesn't stay in place outside us, leaving us untouched and pure. I never feel more despondent than when I discover that evil has managed to invade me and my family. It is not just *out there*, but it is *in here*, closer than my own heartbeat. What is even worse, I've discovered that I am sometimes a willing partner in sin. Evil and I don't mix like oil and water; we're more like sugar and water. Not always, thank God, but enough to make me nod agreement when I read, "Let any one who thinks that he stands take heed lest he fall" (I Cor. 10:12).

Evil is everywhere, and we'll only be saved from its taking over in our lives if we understand how horrible it is. It's fatal to begin accepting evil in our world, or in ourselves. Once we stop struggling against it, we're dead.

I nearly drowned once. I won't bore you with all the embarrassing details, except to say that after I went down a few times, I began to give up, and I found to my amazement that it's possible to breathe under water. I stopped struggling. And that's when I started dying. Obviously someone else thought it would be better if I resumed breathing in the more ordinary way and pulled me to safety. The point is, it's possible to drown in evil too. It's possible to accept it and even to enjoy it. But we need to see evil for what it really is. Chapters 4 through 11 of Genesis help us do that.

In these chapters we find the beginning of *now*—the beginning of *our* age. We don't live in the Garden of Eden; we live East of Eden where sin and death have taken over. I used to think God had exaggerated when He said to Adam, "The day you eat of that tree you will surely die" (cf. Gen. 2:17). I used to think Adam didn't die; he lived. Now I know he *didn't* live; he died all right. When we rebelled against God, we fell backward into the embrace of death.

Did you notice that once Satan crawled into paradise, human life became cheap? That's the way evil operates. It's bound to end in death. Every time. Today when sin and evil, sometimes even death, are portrayed as exciting, alluring, and fascinating, we have to read these chapters frequently. When I read them, I see what sin really is, and it's not what Steve Martin says it is.

I also see God's reaction, and that's important too. It's a reaction of judgment and salvation. The single great theme of the Bible is God's redemption. But that's not all that's in the Bible. The Bible also speaks clearly about God's judgment.

The flood is the great event of judgment in the Old Testament. There is some question whether it was global, but there can be no question that it was a total destruction of the region where the destiny of creation was being worked out. In that place, where great families and nations were growing, large clans of murderers and adulterers—and tinsmiths and rock musicians too—in that region, where only one family finally emerged as

God's righteous people, there the waters of judgment came thundering down.

It's hard now to read the chapters telling of this destruction in such a way that the fear of God gets pounded into our bones. But that's the way we must read it; else we'll be foolish about sin. We are inclined to make jokes about sin sometimes. We can become so accustomed to it that we nestle up to it and savor its taste. Some sins are chocolate-covered, tasty morsels. At least they are presented that way.

The flood is the astonishingly dramatic announcement that no matter how nice, or neat, or cute sin may appear to be, all sin finally brings a reaction from God that leaves human beings flailing around in distress. When we read this material, we have to feel the deadly chill that encircles those upon whom God has turned His back.

I say, it's hard to read the flood report *that* way. The flood record has been "played with" so much that Noah and his ark have become symbols of a great fairy tale. The animals walking two-by-two have become the worldwide symbol of a zoo. The story of the flood has become a classic in children's storybooks. Sunday school teachers love to tell it, and kids listen wide-eyed.

Wide-eyed, indeed. Our eyes must widen now as we think of the reality of judgment. Judgment is real. The wrath of God is real. Hell is real. And finally it all falls on sin and on the sinner. It would fall on me, too, except Jesus has created an ark of safety for me at Calvary.

And this is the great, joy-giving fact the Genesis record of the flood finally leaves us with: The God of judgment has created a way of escape from judgment. The same God who sent water on the creation which had abandoned Him also sent a special person to make salvation possible.

Often we speak too easily of *Noah's* ark. It was not Noah's ark; it was God's ark. Noah was God's man. And Noah's family became the family God chose to return beauty and goodness to the world people had succeeded in corrupting through and through.

So it was God who judged, and it was God who saved. God gave the command to build. God gave the command to the animals to congregate. God gave the command to enter. God closed the door. Then He broke open the fountains of the deep, and rain like a waterfall came from the heavens. And there, riding the surface of water which stood above the mountain peaks, the ark of safety gently rolled in the swells. We have a hundred curious questions about all this. And some wonder whether a strange residue of rotting wood on a Turkish mountain is the remains of that old ark. No matter. The important thing to remember about all this is that the God whose judgment is real is the God who makes salvation possible.

There can be little doubt that the flood actually occurred. It's intriguing to notice that many cultures preserve stories that are similar in their flood mythologies. (Rev. Isaac Jen, Chinese language pastor of the Back to God Hour, once told me, "Oh yes, we Chinese have the story of the flood in our native religion too.") In none of those myths do the majestic fury of the Almighty and the wonder of His grace emerge as they do in the Genesis record. But all the nations have noted this catastrophe.

After the roar of the flood, there is a quiet new beginning. In the new beginning, we see once more the great intentions of the Almighty. There, on the mountainside, God established a covenant with Noah and his family. Think of it—after washing away humanity and all their works, God reached out and entered again into partnership with them.

Covenant, as I have said before, is crucial for an understanding of the Bible. God is a covenant-making God; it must be central to His nature, for here, as human history begins again, the first thing God does is enter into covenant with Noah. But look closely. He makes it with Noah *and with all living things.* He makes a covenant, in fact, with His creation, the object of His love. Humanity is important, but not just in itself; humanity is important because people represent everything else God has made. So Noah appears in Genesis 9 as the one who represents all living beings.

Genesis 9 is the first time we can see the various parts of a covenant. There is a promise here. There are commands here. And there is a sign here—the sign of a rainbow. That's the way covenants always are.

After the flood, after all the devastation, God comes to us again with arms outstretched, inviting us to work with Him in repairing His great world. When I look at humanity before the flood, wallowing around in sinfulness, I wonder what good could come from the human race. And then, when it's all over, I see God coming once more to take our hands and to make us His partners. Then I'm proud to be His child, and I really *do* want to work with Him.

The beginning of now. Really, that's what we have in these remarkable chapters—Genesis 4 through 11. As these chapters come to a close, we see the harsh stirrings of rebellion against heaven as construction begins on the tower city. I shudder as I read it. But God will not forget His covenant. He will see the rainbow sign and remember. He will make salvation possible once more. Just wait.

Suggested Bible Readings

God promises Abraham a land, not for himself but for his descendants. That's why the humanly impossible son of promise is so central to the Abraham story. Abraham has to believe that "the Lord will provide" and that "for God nothing will be impossible."

Genesis 12, 16, 17, 18:1-15, 21, 22; Luke 1:26-37

CHAPTER FOUR

Sands of the Seashore People

I know a man who worked for years in down-town Chicago. He grew to love the city. He found a special excitement in getting on the train and heading for "the loop" each day. After he retired, the thing he missed most was the city. Before long, he announced he'd taken a part-time job with an agency in the loop—not for the money, but to recover that special joy of heading downtown.

It's hard to make comparisons, I know, especially when they stretch across thousands of years; but Abraham from Ur and my friend from Chicago have much in common, I think.

Abraham lived on the other side of Christ about the same number of years that we live on this side of Him. And he lived in a city he knew well, Ur of the Chaldees, a marvelous place.

Writing about it in his book, *The Bible as History*, Werner Keller says that 1500 years before Nebuchadnezzar boasted about his Babylon, the citizens of Ur were living in spacious two-story villas, with thirteen or fourteen rooms in each. According to Keller, Abraham was "no simple nomad...but a son of a great city of the second millennium B.C." I have a feeling that Abraham never forgot the wonder of the city for the New Testament describes his vision of the glorious future as "the city which has foundations, whose builder and maker is God" (Heb. 11:10).

We're accustomed to hearing stories about Abraham, and we've learned to think of Abraham as interesting, but remote. There is little to connect his life to ours. But the New Testament declares that if we believe in Christ, we are Abraham's children (Gal. 3:7,29). In other words, the stories about Abraham are stories about *our father.*

That's an astonishing and, I think, fundamental principle taught in the Bible: Those who believe in Jesus are, because of their faith, children of Abraham.

If you're willing to think about Abraham as your father—as a person like you and me, with friends and family and a home—you may discover that we are alike.

Consider Ur, his city. Abraham was a person much like the modern city dweller, at least when he started out. What worried or irritated or pleased him in his city is probably what worries, irritates, and pleases us in our cities today. The problems and joys of city life have remained remarkably similar over the years.

Or look at Abraham "the sinner." Think of the way he acted with the pagan rulers Pharaoh and Abimelech ("Tell them you're my sister, Sarah").

And remember Abraham's relation to false religion—that, too, is something like ours. Ur of the Chaldees was a thriving metropolitan city and, like all such cities, the false religion that dominated Mesopotamia was woven into everything that occurred there. The city was dotted with ziggurats, Babel-like towers reaching toward the sky. Abraham's father and his uncle were fond of ziggurats and worshiped the false gods they symbolized. So did Abraham, I suppose, until God came and said that He should leave everything and go to Canaan, a land he knew nothing about. In terms of basic characteristics Ur was a modern town and Abraham was a modern man; when we identify with him, we are not engaging in a useless exercise but equipping ourselves for living a God-fearing life today.

I must identify with Abraham. With Abraham begins the religion of which I'm a part. I love this man. I would like to shake his hand and slap him on the back and say, "I'm with you." Because I am. With Abraham, God begins the religion I know. The religion I profess and practice now that I believe in Jesus has made me one of Abraham's descendants—one of the "sands of the seashore" people.

I don't mean to suggest that being a child of Abraham and understanding his religion simply involves shaking hands with the old patriarch and slapping him on the back. What excites me is that the same religion I practice today got its shape and substance as God dealt with my good father. With Abraham, we finally discover the full meaning of *covenant*.

The seventeenth chapter of Genesis tells how the covenant agreement God made with Abraham was finalized. And although *we* may not think it's all so clear, when God came to Abraham and told him He would make a covenant with him, surely Abraham knew what God was talking about. Abraham knew all about covenants because he lived in a region where covenants were very common. Scholars have lately pointed out that the Hittite kings customarily made treaties with their vassal subjects, and these treaties had pretty much the same *form* as did the covenant God made with His people. A king would promise to protect his subjects in return for obedience. When a covenant was agreed upon, it would be sealed with a sign of some kind—often a sacrifice.

I need to emphasize that the world in which Abraham lived was highly developed. When Abraham traveled to Haran (after he left Ur and before he went south into Canaan), he moved through highly developed cultural centers. Haran is near ancient Mari, where a large and magnificent palace has been uncovered. In the world he traveled, Abraham learned of endless treaties that bound people to rulers who promised protection and advantage.

In that setting God came to Abraham. Like earthly kings, God promised Abraham protection in return for obedience. But *unlike* earthly kings, God also promised that Abraham was to become the father of a multitude of nations! What king could make *such* a covenant? Only one—the King of kings! Indeed, one way to understand God's promise to Abraham is that the King of kings comes to Abraham and says, "I'll make of you...a king."

What strikes me about the true religion revealed in the Bible is *the promise of God*. True religion is trusting God's promises. God promised Abraham the impossible: a land that he had no claim to and billions of children by a wife who was barren. Later, after God gave the son of miracle, Isaac, He told Abraham to sacrifice his child. God did *not* make reasonable promises to Abraham;

He consistently promised things that would require miracles if they were to be accomplished.

It's no different for us, really. God comes to us with His unreasonable promises. He promises victory over the grave. He promises eternal life in the heavenly city. There is no way that these can be accomplished except by God's miracles. But in Christ Jesus all promises of God are made possible (II Cor. 1:20). He has already accomplished the miracles for Jesus through His resurrection and ascension; someday He will accomplish them for us. All we must do is believe His promises as Abraham did. We must believe God's promises so fully that we are willing to spend ourselves entirely in His service. We must not only *have* faith; we must *live* by faith. Faith and obedience are so closely united in the Bible that anyone who *lives* in disobedience to God must be doubted when he or she claims to *have* faith. Obedience and faith are so closely united that God's covenant always says how obedience must be expressed.

But now a word of caution: Some people who've wanted to be known as children of Abraham have mistakenly concluded that they could become righteous before God by being obedient. They wanted to mint some coin of obedience they could use to pay for their sins. May I just say now, and we will have to talk about this later, that our righteousness is *given* to us; we don't *earn* it. The Bible is very explicit about this: Abraham believed God and it was "reckoned to him" (meaning, his account was paid) for righteousness (Rom. 4:1-5). Faith and works are intimately connected, but we do not earn our righteousness with our obedience. Our righteousness is, always, a gift.

Abraham, the covenant man, had a beginning of that obedience. He recognized that God was his King and he was God's servant, and so he did what God commanded. As a parent he circumcised his children because they, too, belonged to the King. The promises were as much theirs as their parents. And today parents who understand the covenant and wish to claim their children for the King still mark their children with the sign of the covenant, baptism.

There are many Christians these days who are reluctant to baptize their children because they believe baptism is a sign of faith. It is not. Baptism is the sign of the covenant. Children of believing parents are to be baptized not because they have faith, but because they are members of *God's* covenant people.

Genesis 11-25—here is the beginning of the very same religion I confess and exercise today. I believe I'm a son of Abraham, just as much as Isaiah was, and even more than Jewish people who reject Jesus Christ are. Through the blood of Jesus, I've entered the race of Abraham. I am uncomfortable with any theology that suggests Jews are special and any view of history that calls Palestine the "holy land." The promises God made to Abraham are being fulfilled today as people of every tribe and kindred and tongue turn to Jesus and believe the great promises of God that have been made in Him.

I believe in Jesus, so Abraham is my father, and my children are special; they are children of the covenant, "sands of the seashore people."

Suggested Bible Readings

Hebrews 11 teaches us that the patriarchs were people of faith. That faith was no passive waiting. Conniving, struggling, striving Jacob illustrates the character of that faith. He gives his new name to the people—the Israelites, those who strive with God.

Genesis 27-33; Luke 18:1-8; Hebrews 11

CHAPTER FIVE

The Religion of Moses

The decision to read the Bible from beginning to end is one thing; actually doing it is something else. Somewhere after the fifteenth chapter of Exodus my own determination usually collapses. I develop a vague uneasiness about the Bible. I recall preachers and Sunday school teachers telling me how wonderful, how inspiring the Bible is, and I begin to wonder if these people have ever read through the Bible themselves. There have been times when I've found chapters of the Old Testament to be more of a *test* of my faith than a *support* for it.

I'm convinced, though, that my breakdown along stretches of the Old Testament is due to my imperfections, not the Bible's, and over the years I've found things growing clearer to me. In fact, I've come to see that I cannot grasp the Christian faith unless I have the material in the first five books of the Bible well in hand. I've found it helpful to think of these books in terms of God's law, God's holiness, God's wrath, and God's man.

There are basically two kinds of laws in Moses' books: first are the big laws, the Ten Commandments; second are hundreds of laws that deal with little, picky activities of life. Some of the "little laws" make good sense—I can understand why a soldier should carry a shovel with him so that he can dig a private latrine every time he needs one (Deut. 23:13). But other "little laws" don't make much sense to me, like the law against mixing two kinds of cloth in a garment.

For a long time I wondered what in the world all these little laws were doing in the Bible. It wasn't that the laws themselves weren't sensible; it's just that I couldn't quite understand why God would come from heaven to give toilet instructions to soldiers.

But now I think I see it. What we have in *all* these laws—"big" and "little"—is God forming a special people for Himself, making a nation out of people who were ignorant, stupid, even savage. The people with whom He began really knew nothing about Him. When Moses came to rescue them, they weren't all that sure they wanted to go with him. Through the wilderness they grumbled and griped, sometimes longing for the food of Egypt. Here was a bumbling nation, rescued from slavery entirely by God's acts; they had done nothing to gain their own freedom. They were God's people, but they'd never read a catechism or confession of faith. It was long before Jesus taught us the meaning of love, and they didn't have the Holy Spirit in their hearts as Christians do today.

So God had to teach them *everything*, even how to walk (Hos. 11:3)! What's so incredible about all this is God did it! God came from heaven to spell it all out—not only in the thunder and smoke of Mount Sinai, but also in the quiet, day-to-day instruction, God patiently made a nation out of a mob. And He did it by giving laws, big ones and little ones, so that even the most ignorant could be a part of His great plan. When I remember this it helps me understand what's happening in these books and how the laws have meaning for my life too.

Since so much of Moses' writing involves law, I mentioned it first. But there are other key ideas that I also meet elsewhere in the Bible. If I can understand these things in Moses' books, it helps me understand them in the rest of Scripture. They are these: God's holiness, God's wrath, and God's man.

Holy is a word which says very little to me, frankly. What's holy in our world anymore? Nothing, really. The only time I hear the word is in some common expletives. But in these books Moses wrote, the word *holy* keeps booming up from the pages. The true God is *holy*. Whether He is on the mountain, or in the ark of the covenant, his *holiness* is like a charged field of force that surrounds Him; no mortal person can even approach the mountain or touch the ark and live. His *holiness* rubs off on sacred tools used in worship, including the great altar where only the purest of fire may burn. Even the high priest's clothes become *holy* (Lev. 21).

The idea of holiness is often associated with fire in the Bible—and that's telling. You can't live without fire, but neither can you live in it. You must treat fire with respect or get burned. It can purify and it can destroy. No wonder that when Moses first heard God's voice, it was coming from a *burning* bush. God Himself is called a "consuming fire" in both the Old and the New Testaments (Deut. 4:24, Heb. 12:29).

The reality of God's holiness awakens the fear which leads to obedience: "Fear God, and keep his commandments" (Eccles. 12:13). On Pentecost, fear fell on every soul and what looked like "tongues of flame" danced on believers' heads. Fear is how we feel when suddenly our adrenal glands shoot a burst of adrenalin into our systems—like when a child darts out in front of a car, and we hit the brakes or swerve just barely in time to avoid him. In that instant fear grips our stomach; an electric sensation shoots along our back and over our scalp and leaves us trembling. Something of this fear is always part of our response to God. As we live with God over a period of time, He graciously removes the initial paralysis of fear. But fear itself is always there because God is holy (I Pet. 1:17).

A wet, shivering man may love his fire—but he's a fool if he doesn't fear what an uncontrolled blaze can do. Similarly, the fear I have for God is not only a response to His holiness, to what He is, but it's also a response to what He can do, to His wrath. And this, too, is dramatically revealed in the material Moses wrote.

If the book of Leviticus is the great revelation of God's holiness, the reality of His wrath burns like a smoldering fury in the pages of Numbers. For me, Numbers is the book that reveals the wrath of God the most. The word "hell" doesn't scare me, but "Numbers" does. In Numbers I see what happens to members of God's covenant people when they rebel. In Numbers I see people who lusted for meat; so God gave it to them, and then He killed them before they brushed their teeth (11:33). I see a man executed for picking up sticks on the sabbath day (15:36). I see fourteen thousand seven hundred people, plus two hundred fifty

23

princes of Israel, plus Korah, Dathan, and Abiram, all destroyed because they tried to undercut the leadership of Moses and Aaron (16:49). I see an Israelite and his Midianite wife thrust through with one sword while they embraced (25:8). Simply remembering the book of Numbers convinces me that it *is* a fearful thing to fall into the hands of the living God. The revelation of God's great wrath, knowing that God punishes even His covenant people, keeps the fear of God alive in me.

But these books aren't simply about God's law, or His holiness and wrath. In a powerful way the pages of at least Exodus through Deuteronomy are dominated by the author: Moses, God's man. I don't understand everything about Moses—his life with Zipporah puzzles me, for example. But Moses is the one who in so may ways gives Christianity its shape, its structure. Let me explain.

First of all, it's with Moses that the tie-in between God's religion and God's Word is set up. Moses is the great writer, but God is the Great Writer through Moses. In the five books of Moses there is some holy confusion regarding just who wrote what. The impression is occasionally given that God actually wrote some things with His own hand. At other times, Moses indicates he very carefully wrote the material himself (Deut. 31:24). However it happened, the big fact that emerges is God's Word is available, present, open to you (Deut. 30:11-14).

Secondly, Moses is closely related to Christ. Moses receives God's revelation because God speaks to him "face to face, as a man speaks to his friend" (Ex. 33:11). Moses writes God's words. Then comes Jesus—like Moses, a prophet (Deut. 18:18). But Jesus does not write God's words; Jesus *is* God's Word made flesh. The New Testament tells us that just as God was near in the revelation He gave to Moses, so Jesus is near us in the Word that is preached to us today (Rom. 10:6-8).

There is a sense in which the Christian faith never gets beyond Moses. The true religion of Moses is not changed in Jesus; it is simply fulfilled. So when we read what Moses wrote, we already read what God wants us to know.

And that brings me to something I haven't mentioned yet. The first five books of the Bible show that Christianity is a covenantal religion. There is that word again, *covenant*. Through

Moses God established the fact that He was the bridegroom and Israel was His bride. All that Moses wrote was designed to make Israel special, to give them a satisfying life. No other nation had a God so gracious or so glorious, and no other nation had the wisdom Israel had received directly from God in the law (Deut. 4:7,8). The law is the great foundation of God's covenant. It is the marriage agreement. I am holy, says God, and you must be holy too. We will go through history together: I, the holy God, with you, my holy people.

In the Pentateuch the promises are made. Here we see the wedding rings exchanged. God will be faithful. Israel must be faithful. Near the end of Deuteronomy God reveals that He knows Israel will be unfaithful (Deut. 31:16). But God sees beyond Israel's unfaithfulness to a cross, and a tomb, and a day of Pentecost. The church born at Pentecost has its roots in the desert Moses crossed, leading God's unlikely people.

There is much more. There is the principle of the sabbath and of the sabbath rest. There is the victorious power of God bringing Israel the victory over Sihon and Og. There is the marvelous explanation that the law of God is fulfilled in love. There is the sad death of Moses on Mt. Nebo's slopes. Surely there is enough here to keep me occupied and astonished until I no longer read Moses' books, but meet him face to face.

Suggested Bible Readings

The words of the covenant in Deuteronomy look to the past, present, and future of Israel. In all these directions there is one absolutely stable, dependable presence—God, the Rock. He is the one foundation on which Israel must build if their national house is to stand.

Deuteronomy 29-34; Matthew 7:13-29

CHAPTER SIX

An Ugly Chapter

Golda Meir, former Prime Minister of the new state of Israel, is reported to have said that Moses really didn't do very well. "He led the Jews all over the oil rich nations of the Middle East," she complained, "and then settled them into the only country where there's no oil at all." Oil or not, the promised land has long been eyed with envy by more than a few of its neighbors. From the time of Moses, it has been a prized piece of real estate, often drenched with the blood of its defenders. The story of its capture by ancient Israel, told in Joshua and Judges, is in some ways one of the ugliest chapters in Israel's history.

So now you know that Joshua and Judges are not my favorite parts of the Bible. They remind me of books on "how the west was won." The story of Joshua is especially bloody, and—so far as Israel itself is concerned—extremely disappointing. In fact, I've come away from it feeling that its major point is this: Human beings don't amount to very much. Only God can make something good come out of their treachery and failure.

No, I don't like wading through all the blood in the book of Joshua. Still, I have to admit that the book does teach me something important: It teaches—in sometimes terrifying ways—God's awesome fury for all false religions. You see, in the conquest of Canaan, God was not only fulfilling His promise to give His people the land, but also justly punishing those who lived there. They had earned their own destruction. Cult prostitution, homosexuality, infanticide, sensuous life-styles, and a host of other evils so pervaded their culture that, sadly, it became necessary for God to totally destroy it.

As I read of the fall of Jericho described in the opening chapters of Joshua, it hits me hard that all this was God's doing, not the people's. The promise was fulfilled and the threat carried out by God alone. It was by God's great miracle that the people got the land, not by their courage or moral stature; as a matter of fact, Israel was more similar to the nations she destroyed than she was different from them. Her people hadn't even settled Canaan before they began taking God pretty much for granted.

But it was God, working through Joshua, who was the great mover and shaker, making Canaan fall and divide. Jericho is the symbol of the way the victory was achieved—silent people walking around the city. It must have been an eerie sight, weird beyond words. Who ever heard of conquering cities by marching *around* them? But the final point was entirely clear: When the trumpet sounded, it was God who gave the victory.

And it was God who made the sun and moon stand still in the great miracle recorded in Joshua 10. When I first heard the story of that miracle, it didn't strike me as all that great. I was a child, then—possibly around five—and the God I believed in could do things like that. But as a little child I had no conception of the universe, and I knew nothing about the solar system delicately balanced on cosmic lines of gravity. I never thought *then* that if God really answered Joshua's prayer, the whole universe would have fallen apart; why, matter itself would have collapsed. When I was older, though, and read the tenth chapter of Joshua again, the words stared me in the face. What should I say about the sun and the moon stationary in the sky while the Amorites were being slaughtered?

I think, now, that Joshua 10 is one chapter we can use to measure our faith. I believe it. And I confess my belief with jubilation and exhilaration greater than when I first believed. I realize now that the issue confronting me here confronts me with each miracle recorded in the Bible. Either God is the God the Bible says He is, or He isn't worth wasting my time with. But the Bible's right: He *is* the Almighty Creator. The sun and the moon are His. And then I am reminded that this history with its miracles is all extremely important. God's giving the land of Canaan to Israel is terribly important. And people who say some parts of the Bible are not their favorite must be very careful how they handle the holy Scriptures.

The book of Judges is a record of Israel's continuous game-playing with the idolatry of nations they had supposedly destroyed. Israel was sworn to faithfulness to her husband —God—but she loved flirting with idols. Several times in the history of the conquest it is noted that, in fact, not all the Canaanites were killed. Some were kept as slaves. In Judges we see the results of this mistake: Heathen tribes sweep across the country God had given His people. In all, the children of Israel look very bad.

And even the judges who were raised up to deliver them are remarkably strange heroes. The one about whom we know most, whose parents and birth and upbringing are carefully recorded, is Samson. In his fights with the Philistines, the large defects of his own character become apparent. He has shrewdness going for him, but basically his personality is weak. It's God, again, who comes off as the deliverer; the warped and broken judges often need more deliverance than they bring.

It has sometimes been pointed out that the Acts of the Apostles does not really describe the work of the apostles at all, but rather the work of the Holy Spirit. The same point can be made about the history we enter in the books of Joshua and Judges. People recede into the background as God steps forward, the all-powerful One working out His purposes in spite of people. We see that people can escape obedience, but they can never escape the God who calls for their obedience. Repeatedly the Bible turns our attention from human failure to God's conquest. It is God's Spirit which suddenly comes upon Samson in Judges 14, and it's God who pulled Samson into His fight with the Philistines (14:4). It's God who sweeps in with judgment when His people step too far out of line—Abimelech, for example, was destroyed by God for the crime he committed against his brothers (Judg. 9:56). But it's also God who never gives up on Israel, even when giving up seems most reasonable.

In these books we see the quality of life deteriorating terribly among the covenant people of God. The nineteenth chapter of Judges illustrates this most graphically—and may be the ugliest, most repulsive chapter in the entire Bible. This is no isolated horror story sensationally told for entertainment or cash. This is a brutal description of the depths to which life in the land of Israel had sunk. These were *God's* people, if you can imagine it. Among them there were no resources left for their own renewal, let alone for the salvation of the world. The great miracle is that God will use Israel so that one day there will come from these treacherous, immoral people a Savior who is Christ the Lord. Next to *that* miracle, making the sun and moon stand still looks easy.

If there is much here that makes a person recoil in horror, there are also elements of these books that give marvelous insights into the souls of ancient people. Deborah's song is magnificent (Judg. 5). I especially like the part in which she describes Sisera's mother. Sisera was a Canaanite general who had been killed by Jael, a women who had driven a tent pin through his skull. When Deborah sings of his defeat and disgrace, she sings about Sisera's mother waiting at the lattice for the return of her son from battle. This is magnificent poetry, and significant too in the way it shows how the people of that day thought. They were not very much different from us.

And I can't help but be impressed by the Midianite kings Zebah and Zalmunna (Judg. 8). Gideon commanded that they be killed, but the young soldier hesitated; he was just a boy. And the sentenced kings looked Gideon in the eye and said, "Come on, kill us yourself. It takes a man to do a man's job" (TEV). Gideon killed them, but there was not all that much difference between the Midianite kings and their executioner. The only difference was that God had chosen Gideon, as He chooses us, by grace alone.

The promises of God are sure. God promised the land to A-braham six hundred years earlier, and God fulfilled His promise. When Joshua planted the bones of Joseph in Schechem, God's people had finally come home.

God gave them the victory, and God alone preserved this faltering nation. Joshua and Judges give no reason for praising Israel, or humanity in general. In chapters often bloody, sometimes depressing, occasionally repulsive, they teach the eternal truth: To God alone be glory.

War and conquest are a brutal business. Utter destruction was needed, not just to win the promised land, but to cleanse it. After the evil had been cast out, the Israelites were to make the land holy. By God's power they accomplished the first step quite well. The second was less successful.

Joshua 5-10; Luke 11:14-26

CHAPTER SEVEN

The Hyphenated Israelite

Part of the world in which I live as a Christian is the fierce, troubled world of David, the great king of Israel. I love the royal images of the book of Hebrews and the sweet hymn of I Corinthians 13. But I also know from my own experience that Christians sometimes live in a rough and tumble world like David's.

When reading through the Bible, I always feel there's a big shift once the book of Judges closes: *People* suddenly become very prominent. There's no book called "Moses," for example, but after Judges we read "Ruth." And it's a long, long way from the sordid conclusion of the book of Judges to the fields where Ruth gleaned and Boaz fell in love. That there could be a story like Ruth's, set during "the days when the judges ruled," is a much needed assurance that not everything within the boundaries of Israel had collapsed completely.

But I must be careful with Ruth; it would be a mistake to think too much about her personal qualities. Though I can learn from her faithfulness and can even be calmed by her tranquil nature, I must remind myself that Ruth's supreme importance is expressed in the way God used her to achieve His great work.

Ruth's story is really Obed's story, David's grandfather's story. Obed was Ruth's son, and Obed was a hyphenated Israelite, a Moabite-Jew. This hyphenated Israelite was David's grandfather and Jesus' great-great-great-...grandfather. Matthew's genealogy of Jesus dwells long enough on this short history for the apostle to mention each of their names: Boaz, Ruth, Obed, Jesse, David.

David—surely the material in Ruth's story, and the two books that carry Samuel's name, must be viewed in terms of David who has no book entitled for him. These books revolve around Israel's monarchy, the establishment of the kingdom. I sometimes feel that David is the only *real* king Israel ever had. Others occupied the throne, indeed, but none of their careers measure up to the *ideal* of the Israelite king. And really, it's the ideal of the king that's most important in the Bible, not the king himself or the land he ruled. We see how important that ideal is when we first see the King, Jesus, and hear Him say, "The kingdom of God is at hand" (Mark 1:15).

Centuries before David, God had described the conduct of the perfect king of Israel: He would rule with a copy of the law of God always at his elbow, and he would read it all the days of his life (Deut. 17:18,19). His kingdom would be peaceful, and the king would be pure, sober, and humble. As the chosen one of God the king would rule wisely, and his people would benefit greatly. Eventually, God chose David to represent this kingdom.

At the center of the biblical material dealing with David is II Samuel 7. In this passage God promises David, "Your house and your kingdom shall be made sure for ever before me; your throne shall be established for ever" (7:16). All of the characteristic marks of the covenant are in this promise to David. The two greatest themes in the Bible, covenant and kingdom, are brought together when God's covenant partner rules the kingdom with justice and mercy. Says David, "The king who rules with justice, who rules in reverence for God, is like the sun shining on a cloudless dawn, the sun that makes the grass sparkle after rain" (II Sam. 23:3,4, TEV).

It's sometimes hard for me to see how the establishment of David's kingdom directly affects me, a Christian living in the twentieth century. But when I read this material closely, and get to know the people involved, I notice that the ideas of covenant, king, and kingdom begin to take on flesh and blood. In a sense, even God takes on flesh and blood here.

Oh, I know God didn't literally take on flesh and blood until Jesus Christ was born. But when I read the book of Samuel, God seems as tangibly there as Saul and Samuel. These people have running conversations with God, and God is surprisingly open and stunningly frank with them. If we're caught short seeing Jesus weeping in front of Lazarus's tomb, what do we think when we hear God tell Samuel, "I'm sorry I chose Saul as king" (cf. I Sam. 15:11)? God, in a real way, takes on "flesh and blood" in this material; He is always present, center stage, interacting with flesh and blood human beings. And it is all presented with sharp, honest realism in these chapters of Scripture.

The kingdom of David was not established smoothly, as if God easily shifted the gears of history and His people slid painlessly from living under the judges to living under kings. The story of the emerging kingdom begins with the tension-filled history of Samuel and Saul.

One could write a novel about Samuel: his splendid youth, his glorious rulership, his inability to face the facts of his own diminished power. (I am always impressed by his scoundrel son Joel, of whom I fervently hope my own mother was ignorant when she chose my name.)

And the monster passions that made Saul a wretched man are reported in great detail in the Bible. We see him bumping along through his mid-life crisis, torn by jealousy and finally succumbing to horrible depression and paranoia.

But standing out from all the others is David. His personality was at the center then, and his kingdom still endures now. Like any other real human being, David had his ups and downs. That sounds trite, but unfortunately that's how life is: We all have our ups and downs, our good days and our bad. At his worst, David is the calculating, treacherous murderer of Uriah, the lustful, selfish potentate who made Bathsheba his wife. No amount of rationalization can explain this deep, determined plunge into sin. I can understand David's desire for Bathsheba, but how David could destroy the valiant, loyal soldier, Uriah, is incomprehensible.

I am more and more impressed by the fact that David was a warrior; I sometimes wonder if we do not tend to downplay this element of his life. When people talk of David, generally, they like to dwell on his being a shepherd king, and they remember his poetic talent. Fine. But the David we meet in Samuel's books is a soldier's soldier.

33

David knew military strategy. He knew deception. He knew camouflage. He knew weapons. He knew the frenzy, even the ecstasy, a soldier feels when he kills in the heat of battle. With his enemies he was ruthless. Can you imagine him making the Moabites lie down and putting two out of every three to death (II Sam. 8:2)?

So the kingdom was established. In battle. With bloodshed. With regiments of soldiers sent to hell. "Jesus shall reign where'er the sun does his successive journeys run"—altogether now, sing it out! What's the relationship between David's and Jesus' reign? One part of the relationship involves fighting. David was a soldier. So was Jesus. Must I be? "Onward Christian soldiers . . . ." I worry when my children play with guns, but I'm pleased when they sing "Onward Christian Soldiers." I'll need a few more years to figure all this out—the role of violence and fighting in our world. How long, for example, can I sit by and let Christ's enemies kill unborn children?

But David was more than a warrior. Think of his mercy and his absolute devotion to a promise; remember his treatment of Mephibosheth, Saul's son whom David reinstated at his own table when he returned to Jerusalem after Absalom's rebellion. I recall David's devotion to justice, his commitment to serve, his willingness to die for the sake of the kingdom. Through all of this it's possible to draw lines from David to Christ.

After looking long and often at David, I've come away with the assurance that more than anything else this man loved and feared God. In his best moments he knew that he lived in the presence of the Almighty—that it was God and God alone who directed his life, and that it was God whom he should serve. In his final estimate of his own life, David played down his personal talents and virtues, and stressed instead that he was God's chosen king.

> O Lord, you give me victory over my enemies and protect me from violent men. And so I praise you among the nations; I sing praises to you. God gives great victories to his king; he shows constant love to the one he has chosen, to David and his descendants forever.
>
> (II Sam. 22:49-51, TEV)

Even David could not guess what Christians today know.

God's promise to establish David's throne forever was sealed many years later in "the city of David," on the night an infant King was laid in Bethlehem's straw. The Spirit promised to David was the Spirit at Christ's baptism and at the Pentecost birth of the church. And we are David's descendants, the ones to whom God "gives great victories" and "shows constant love."

Seeing David, we recall there is no other religion like the Christian faith, for there is no other book like the Bible. It is utterly realistic about people and about God, and about God and His creatures together. If only I can be as realistic about myself! If only I can remember that every morning when I get up I stand in the presence of the same God Saul and David faced! Like the kings of old, I live before God. And I will be safe so long as I stay very close to the King I met at Calvary.

Suggested Bible Readings

It was hard being a foreigner in Israel. It was like being a dog under the master's table, begging scraps. But Ruth accepted that position out of love for her mother-in-law. She became one of the most openly praised women in the Bible. Jesus praised a woman like Ruth also.

Ruth; Matthew 15:21-28

CHAPTER EIGHT

Staying Sane While Reading

The decline of the kingdom of Israel (including Judah) is very important in Bible history—so important that the sorry record is played not once, but twice. Two volumes named Kings and two more under the title of Chronicles detail the fatal plunge of the kingdom; these books take up more than ten percent of the Bible, 144 pages in the edition I use most often. They are, almost page-by-page, testimonies to human failure. While we need to know the history in these books to understand why the kingdom collapsed, and we need to know about the collapse to understand the cross of Christ—still, reading these chapters can actually challenge our sanity.

I'm serious about this. And I'm serious about it because of Tony, a sensitive man who's tasted life and found it sour, who's dissatisfied not only with other people, but with himself. Tony claims that most people he knows are hateful and selfish; quietly he admits that he is too. In his better moments Tony makes cynical jokes about life; but in other moments he becomes terribly depressed and wonders if it would hurt to die.

From everything Tony's told me, I think he wants God to help him get through each day. He's a searching, inquiring man. As a part of that search he reads the Bible. And when he reads the history of Israel's rejection of God and all that happened as a result, he's shattered. He calls me up, or comes over, and we talk. I tell him that the God we meet in Kings and Chronicles (and all the rest of the Bible) is the God who finally revealed

Himself in Jesus Christ. And then Tony looks at me and shakes his head in near disbelief. He can't believe that the God revealed in these chapters is the God who so loved the world that He gave His Son to die for its redemption.

I can sympathize with Tony. Anyone who reads Kings and Chronicles, and really listens to what's being said there, *should* be shaken. I am, and I think you should be too. We should all feel decent horror when we hear that thousands of people have, for *any* reason, died.

I'd like to tell you four things I keep in mind when reading these books. If I forget these items, the material doesn't help me very much—in fact, it hurts me in much the same way it hurts Tony. But when I keep my whole-Bible perspective, I stay sane while reading and actually learn from Kings and Chronicles.

(I don't mean to give the impression that if you only think the way I think, you'll be safe. Perhaps you need your own set of guidelines. But, for what they're worth, here are mine.)

First, I'm reminded powerfully in these books that God is faithful: When He says He's going to do something, He does it. He never makes an idle promise or a hollow threat. God promised David that his kingdom was going to last forever. (II Sam. 7), and later He repeated that promise to Solomon. But always the promise was hinged on obedience—and to those who heard the promise clearly heard the need for obedience. Listen, for example, to I Kings 6:11;12 (TEV):

> The Lord said to Solomon, "*If you obey all my laws and commands*, I will do for you what I promised your father David. I will live among my people Israel in this Temple that you are building, and I will never abandon them."

The condition of obedience was so clear in God's promise that even the heathens understood it. God told Solomon that if the heathen saw the temple in ruins and asked each other why, they'd answer:

> "It is because [the people] abandoned the Lord their God, who brought their ancestors out of Egypt. They gave their allegiance to other gods and worshiped them. That is why the Lord has brought this disaster on them."
>
> (I Kings 9:9, TEV)

When we hear the promises of God, we tend to hear only what

37

we want to hear. Solomon did that. So did all the kings that followed him. In fact, all the people of Israel ignored God when they wanted to. Because of their deafness to God's full promise, the nation went into exile. Even then there was grace:

> But the Lord was kind and merciful to them. He would not let them be destroyed, but helped them because of his covenant with Abraham, Isaac, and Jacob. He has never forgotten his people.   (II Kings 13:23, TEV)

What God wants me to understand, I think, is the seriousness of His promises and the absolute consistency with which He operates. He wants me to listen closely when He speaks. He comes with promises, promises, promises; and He is faithful, faithful, faithful. . . .

The second thing I remember when reading Kings and Chronicles is that we live in a very "moral" universe, one in which sin is eventually punished.

I know it's been said that the wages of sin are death, but who believes it? Apparently I don't really believe it since I behave as if I can fudge a little on my favorite sins and still escape death. We are all living in an age when the universe does not *seem* moral; evil people are doing evil things and are evidently getting away with them. It seems like justice is absent. Big nations like the United States can bloody the Vietnam countryside because of American stupidities, cover the whole thing over with fancy rhetoric, and then go on as if the war never happened. Business, government, even religion are shot through with fraud. To the extent that I am a child of my age, I doubt that the wage for sin is death because I doubt that the universe is moral.

The centuries of Israel's history spread out on the pages of Kings and Chronicles show me now utterly mistaken I am about sin. Sin brings death, no matter whether a person comes from Judah, Naphtali, Canada, or the States. This is the meaning of the bloodshed that makes these books so indescribably ugly. At one time a hundred thousand Syrians were killed (I Kings 20:29); at another, a hundred eighty-five thousand Assyrians died (II Kings 19:35); at still another, whole armies turned on each other, and in a frenzy of bloodletting all were destroyed (II Chron. 20:24). These slaughters are mind-boggling. In the stench that rose from the battlefield, in the treachery that brought one king after another to his downfall, we observe that God does not tolerate injustice and rebellion against Him. This *is* a moral universe because it was created as it is now governed—by a fiercely moral God.

But wait a minute: God's not only moral—He's also gracious. He gives us an avenue of escape after sin—repentance. Repentance is so powerful that it can ward off judgment. I remember *that* too when I read that Ahab, who sinned more than any other king of Israel, received God's grace simply for humbling himself in repentance (I Kings 2:28, 29).

The third thing I recognize, as I walk through the blood-soaked territory of Kings and Chronicles and I see the smoldering ruins of a nation, is the corruption and power of false religion. God's chosen child, Israel, fell under judgment and into exile. Why? Because Israel loved idols. It's so deadly simple we tend to ignore it.

And, frankly, we can't afford to ignore it because false religion is on every side of us today. Israel was tempted by cult prostitution involving men and women—modern gods still love such prostitution. Ancient people stripped their children and laid them on burning altars; modern children are snuffed out by selfish parents on the altar of abortion. Those who survive sometimes become favorite playthings in pornography, and are more likely to be physically (including sexually) abused by their parents or guardians than by any stranger. Kings and Chronicles aren't pretty; neither is modern prostitution, abortion, pornography, or child abuse. What's common to both, though, is false religion and its devastating consequences. We do not have to enjoy these facts, but we have to believe them. Else we'll become like Israel: "They worshiped worthless idols and became worthless themselves..." (II Kings 17:15, TEV).

Finally, as I read this material, I try to discipline myself to emphasize the bright spots. Between all the bloodshed and judgment on these pages, amid all the horror that accompanies the deterioration of God's chosen people, there are marvelous bursts of light. Among a score of depraved kings are decent men like King Asa and King Hezekiah. After years of idolatry, King Josiah led the people in a rediscovery of the law, a national repentance, and a great reform. On these pages we meet the prophets Elijah and Elisha. During this time the office of prophet was developed—with Elisha himself the head of a school of prophets. God's testimony was not extinguished. In the message of the prophets was the hope that the idolatry which had the nation in a death grip would not ultimately gain the upper hand. That same message rings through Isaiah, Jeremiah, and others we'll study later, prophets who lived during the time described in Kings and Chronicles.

In reading any part of the Bible, but especially books like Kings and Chronicles, I remember Jesus. I know more about Jesus than I know about kingdom collapse. My questions about sin and judgment in Kings and Chronicles are finally answered when I stand at Calvary. There God punished sin once and for all, in Jesus. And in Jesus I know that I can escape the hell depicted so brutally in Kings and Chronicles. The last word about God is not found there; it's found in the Word, Jesus. If I could help Tony see *that*, then he might also see that the God who comes to me in Jesus is the God I meet in Kings.

Part of God's grace is that He's honest with us. From the very beginning, He's told us the truth about sin and punishment ("If you eat of the tree . . ."). I believe He gives us Kings and Chronicles because He is gracious; He wants us to be shaken, and broken, and repentant. He wants us to flee to Jesus.

Suggested Bible Readings

Fire from heaven—that could be the motto for the violent time of the old kingdom. God's fire countered the fire and sword on earth. But it's completely inappropriate for the new kingdom of Christ.

II Kings 1-5; Luke 9:51-62

CHAPTER NINE

The Psalm Problem

"*I* have to know Psalm 23 by heart next Friday!"

For many of us, such assignments were our first impression of the Psalms. Twenty-three was easy to learn, but 119 was hopelessly long. Back and forth we roamed through the book of Psalms, memorizing a verse here and a passage there. Our goal, it seemed, was recitation, and if we performed well we were rewarded. Already then, you see, we were developing what would later prove to be "the psalm problem"—the fact that we've not learned to be moved or genuinely inspired by the Bible's poems.

I should probably confess that I'm rarely excited by *any* poetry. I admire what poets can do with words and meters, but I'm just not lifted or inspired by much poetry. Frankly, I'm ashamed of this. I know my lack of excitement over good poetry is a reflection on me, not on the poetry.

When it comes to the Psalms, though, the problem is even greater. After all, there are one hundred and fifty psalms! That's a lot of poetry! Yet I know these psalms are part of God's inspired Word and are loved by Christians the world over. They *should* excite me too. I'm really troubled that they often don't.

Oh, there are some exceptions. Psalms 40, and 90, and 96 are capable of moving me deeply. I cannot read them without sensing their beauty, strength, and truth. But if you survey all one hundred and fifty psalms, the percentage that startle and awaken me with strong emotion is low. I don't believe I've ever been moved, for example, when I read: "Vindicate me, O Lord, for I have walked in my integrity, and I have trusted in the Lord without wavering" (Ps. 26:1).

One thing that's recently been helpful to me is reading the Psalms in new translations. I enjoy Today's English Version which gives the Psalms a muscular, dynamic quality. I like the Jerusalem Bible's Psalms, and the translation in the New International Version. This is a beginning, a help; but it doesn't get at the root of the problem.

I think I'm getting closer to that root when I finally admit, reluctantly, that not every single part of the Bible is equally exciting to every Christian. When I consider the Psalms, for example, I must remember that this songbook has served the people of God for many, many centuries. Some of these songs were sung by the faithful as Israel and Judah collapsed. The seven thousand who never bowed their knees to Baal must have used them. Some psalms were written by returning exiles, ecstatic because the temple service was being restored. This was the songbook of pious Jews during Jesus' day. This was Jesus' psalter, even on the cross when He made the heartbreaking cries of Psalm 22 His own. The early church listened intently to Psalm 2 as the fury of developing persecution mounted. Down through the centuries, these songs have belonged to *all* the faithful—they are not my private collection, intended for my individual excitement.

What's more, I'm far removed from the original settings of the Psalms. Unlike David, I've never had a Philistine king threaten to destroy me; I've only had a flat tire on the expressway at midnight in zero-degree weather. Unlike David, I've never had my wife reprimand me for dancing indecently; I've only heard my wife's anger when I allowed our garage to become a disaster area. So I have to understand that some circumstances behind the Psalms are foreign to my own experience; I can't expect each reference to speak directly to me.

Perhaps the major single difference between the world in which the Psalms were written, and the world in which I read those Psalms today, is the day-to-day reality of warfare. The contexts of many psalms, and references in even more of them, involve battle—a fight is about to break out, or is going on, or is just finished. The conscious presence of an enemy broods over the Psalms. And those who wrote these poems often worked in the quiet which came just before the battle, feeling as I do on a sultry, still, tornado-warning day; there's something evil brewing, and I can feel it in the air.

Writing now, I do remember times when the Psalms spoke to me, moving me as they've seldom moved me since. I remember reciting Psalm 91 in 1952, while marching as part of the infantry. I kept repeating, "A thousand may fall dead beside you...but you will not be harmed," and in an awful moment of truth I blurted out, "Lord, Lord, please let it be true for me."

I remember the way our whole church in Cutlerville, Michigan, read the same Psalm (91) on D-Day, 1944. We knew our fathers, sons, brothers, and friends were wading ashore in Europe. We also knew that some would not hit the beach until the waves washed in their bodies. I was greatly moved by Psalm 91 that Sunday.

And I remember Staff Sargeant Charles Van Poolen writing home from Europe, asking our congregation to sing "Under His wing I am safely abiding," based on Psalm 91. We sang it in church, but he died in combat anyway.

I think now that Psalm 91 speaks best to those who want to live and soon may die. That's when it spoke to me, and my church, and Staff Sargeant Charles Van Poolen.

And when I remember all this, I realize that one reason the Psalms don't often catch and shake me *now* is that my life is so calm, so safe and peaceful. This is true because I'm not in a staging area waiting for orders to move out and fight a war; but it's also true because I don't always sense the *spiritual* battle going on all around me. And it's very important to be aware of the spiritual qualities in the battlefield images of the Psalms.

David did not view his enemies as people who merely disliked or offended *him*—they were *God's* enemies. The battles presented in the Psalms are described as parts of the universe-wide battle between God and Satan. And that battle still continues, even though it entered a different phase at Calvary. The "Battle of Calvary" was the decisive victory. But the mopping up operations will go on so long as the devil, wounded now, goes around like a roaring lion.

The Psalms spoke to me when I could sense the battle, especially when I began to concentrate on the part that I might have to play. It's my easy, leisurely, compromising life that makes me unresponsive to the Psalms. They are out of place in my life, like the Marine Hymn being blared through a sleepy library.

The reason the Psalms seldom break my heart or lift me up, I'm afraid, is because my faith is not what it should be, or could be, or even will be someday. The Psalms were written at the *peak* of faith, at those special times when God's children saw themselves and their world as they really were. They saw through the bright eyes of faith how small they were (like a puff of wind), how desperately they needed forgiveness and protection, and how much they depended on the Word of God. If only I had their clear vision, their faith, I know their psalms would reach my soul.

But I should not despair. I have realized that we must go on, day after day, learning what faith means. In joy and in sorrow, in victory and defeat, in eager youth and trembling old age . . . our faith grows, and the Psalms *gradually* become our songbook. It doesn't happen overnight.

I should not despair, for the Psalms, like the rest of the Bible, have been written by the Spirit of God so that our faith may grow. In the very frustrations we experience when we read the Psalms, we may be assured that God is moving us forward and upward. In the moment we feel we cannot properly understand the Psalms because we have lost the sense of the enemy's presence, God uses the Psalms to alert us that our enemy is near. In the moment we do not understand the Psalms because our own lives are too complacent and lazy, God uses those Psalms to challenge us to new dedication and new willingness to take risks for Him. In the moment that we do not understand the Psalms because our faith is weak, God pours His strength into us through those same Psalms.

But I should not despair. God, after all, does not ask us to be wildly enthused by every word or chapter or verse in the Bible. He doesn't say, "Ignore my Word if it doesn't get to you in some emotional way." He simply doesn't guarantee that we'll be excited by every passage. He *does* ask—in fact, He demands—that

44

we listen to every word, and believe, and show our faith in obedience.

Suggested Bible Readings

The Psalms give us striking images and descriptions of the faith life. God is a shepherd, a fortress, a healer of broken bones. The believer is a sheep, a snared bird, a little less than God. Those psalm images fill the New Testament also. Jesus Himself used one to describe Himself as the Good Shepherd.

Psalms 8, 23, 51, 91, 116; John 10:1-18

CHAPTER TEN

"A" Is for Adultery

There are few more beautiful places in the world than the southern coast of France near Monte Carlo. But during the dismal winter of 1978-79, this otherwise sunswept region had its share of dreary days. For reasons that still aren't clear, an unexpected fascination with the past invaded the cafes and hotels of the great resort cities: People became interested in, of all things, New England *Puritans!*

Anthony Burgess, the man who gave us *Clockwork Orange*, visited the coast of France during the "Puritan revival." He describes a French rock group which composed their own music, using lyrics borrowed from early American Puritan preachers— "My Deare Lord, I know not what to say . . . ." In an attempt to understand these singers and others like them, Burgess read Jonathan Edwards's most awesome sermon, "Sinners in the Hands of an Angry God," a bit of reading which could put the fear of God into almost anybody.

As Burgess continued his observations, he became particularly interested in one young man. He was a producer of tee shirts who had recently become interested in the life of Cotton Mather, the great Puritan preacher who wrote no less than four hundred forty-four immense books. The young man's shirts are made of (what else?) cotton, and his slogans are simple. According to Burgess, the most recent proposal of this tee shirt producer is a shirt decorated with a simple scarlet A.

Ah, yes . . . the big A. For those who've read *The Scarlet Letter*, the brilliant red *A* can refer to only one thing: adultery. In Nathaniel Hawthorne's book it was Hester Pryne who wore it, condemned because she bore her child out of wedlock and kept secret the identity of the clergyman who caused her downfall. For Ms. Pryne, as we would surely call her now, the scarlet *A* was a scornful brand insuring her community disdain. But nowadays, if tee shirts carried that brutal sign, I'm certain they'd be worn proudly; in our time, it's almost impossible to commit adultery in a way that would cause community rejection.

As a matter of fact, there's very little community rejection for *any* kind of sin these days. Television, music, movies, magazines—all tell us sin is sensational, or at the very least, laughable. In clever slogans and cute statements, tee shirts and bumper stickers reassure us: "Don't worry about sin, because you can't." Can't sin, that is.

Those who think this way should know that, as Jonathan Edwards would tell them, the eternal flames are already licking at their ankles. The story Jesus told about the Pharisee and the publican leads to the inescapable conclusion that if you don't say, "Oh God, be merciful to me, a sinner," you're doomed. Neither of the two men is a stranger to us. The one, thoroughly at home with religious things, congratulates God on how well they get along together. The other, thoroughly familiar with his sin, is heartbroken. Jesus said the heartbroken man went home made right with God while the proud man left the temple heading for hell.

Brokenheartedness over sin—it's essential if the cool refreshment of the gospel is to flow over our lives. But we don't have to wait for the New Testament to learn that truth. Look at Psalm 51. Here is comfort found deep in the Old Testament. Here is one psalm which unfailingly pulls me up out of the mire of my sin.

Yes, this is the same person who just one short chapter ago admitted that the Psalms sometimes leave him cold! Psalm 51 doesn't. It gets to me every time. I can't escape it, nor do I want to. Like David, its author, I sin horribly, I hurt with guilt, and I need my Father to take me by the hand and say, "I forgive." David's experience becomes my own. It must.

David's sin, like my own, was no little thing. For a time David had been treating adultery like a king's sport; it amused him, as a scarlet letter might amuse some foolish sinners of our age. Then David heard Nathan's warning that God thinks of adultery not as a sport, but as an insult. At last, he saw the truth and turned to God in confession.

In the process of brokenhearted confession, David learned a lot about sin. "In sin did my mother conceive me," he admits, and I silently agree, knowing that from the moment of my birth, I'm involved with sin. Forget those sweet thoughts about innocent little children and take the realistic line of the form for infant baptism: "Infants are without their knowledge partakers of the condemnation in Adam." With David, I have to agree that my sin is no accident; it's rooted in the way I am by nature. Something dreadful and corrupting happened back there in Genesis 3. David knew it and I know it today. It's just a fact—a depressing, dismal, ugly fact—I not only commit sin, but I am a sinner. I was born that way.

David also teaches me to see sin for what it really is: an insult to the God who made me and who saved me. David says, "I have sinned against you—only against you..."(51:4, TEV). Sometimes I want to shout, "David, what about Uriah whom you murdered? What about Bathsheba whom you violated? Wasn't your sin against *them* rather than against God?" But now I think I understand. David certainly did sin against other people, but he was dead right in realizing that his malicious treatment of people was a sin against God, their Maker, against the God who made the human race and surrounded it with His command to love Him and our neighbor. If there were no God or no moral law, life would become a jungle. Killing and adultery might yield some inconveniences, but they would not be wrong in themselves. But there *is* a God and there is a moral law. And so I learn from Psalm 51 that every time I sin against my wife or my children or my fellow workers or whomever, I sin against my God.

Psalm 51 teaches us about our sin; but, thank God, it doesn't stop there. Contaminated, disqualified by shame, David threw himself on the love and mercy of our Lord. From Psalm 51, I see with great relief that it is not the angry God of Jonathan Edwards who summons me, but my loving Father to whom I say,

"Be merciful to me, O God, because of your constant love." My confession of sin is not forced from my lips by a brutal God; it comes gently, naturally, when I remember His lovingkindness. I am not begging a torturer to stop beating me; I'm saying, "Father, forgive..."

When I think of the slimy sin out of which David was crawling when he sent this prayer of repentance heavenward, I'm astonished at what he prayed for. David does not sound the note of the prodigal son, "Just make me one of your hired servants." Instead, he asks for full restoration, for perfect washing, a sound of gladness and joy, for the healing of every broken bone. "Give me again the joy that comes from your salvation, and make me willing to obey you," (51:12, TEV). Psalm 51 shows a king taking hold of *his* King's covenant promises. Human sin is despicable; it's enough to make a person weep in eternal shame. True. But the grace of God is greater than all our sin, not only bringing forgiveness, but also creating a pure heart and a new spirit in us. Because of God's good grace, the possibilities for renewal and growth as a Christian are enormous.

And the way this happens is so clear in this very valuable psalm—it all happens through repentance. This is the great message that stays with me as I lay the psalm down, and it's a message which can bring about new life in multitudes of people. God wants brokenhearted people. Only brokenhearted people have a chance with Him. So David says, "My sacrifice is a humble spirit, O God; you will not reject a humble and repentant heart" (51:17, TEV).

Frankly, God has a soft heart for repentance. God always notes it, and He saves people who do it. There are lots of examples. But here is the simple statement: God will not reject a humble and repentant heart. That was Jesus' point when He told of the Pharisee and publican in the temple. That explains the confession of the apostle Paul, the least of the apostles because he persecuted the church: "Christ came into the world to save sinners, and I am the worst of them."

"I am the worst of them." "O God, be merciful to me, a sinner." I know that when I sincerely pray that way, God will come to me with the lifting power of His great mercy. I don't know your sin, but I know mine; and if I had time enough and grace enough, I could write about it as meaningfully as St. Augustine wrote of his sins (in his book, *Confessions*). For now, I have no book. But I have Psalm 51, and it is enough to coax out my own confessions.

Suggested Bible Readings

God is righteous and just. That's frightening to the wicked. It's consoling to the repentant. Luther said, "It is God's justice which justifies us and saves us." He found that in Paul's epistles. It's also taught in the Psalms.

Psalms 10, 37, 73, 92, 94; Luke 18:9-17

CHAPTER ELEVEN

Every Man, Every Woman

The suicide rate among young people is rising rapidly; it now trails only accident as the most prevalent cause of death among teenagers. People, it appears, are catching on early. It used to take longer for men and women to discover that life is a trap from which death is the only escape. Now they find out by the time they're seventeen.

There is, I believe, a time in each of our lives when we would like to call back the day of our conception, cancel it, and take ourselves out of history. We hear ourselves say, "If I'd never been born, I wouldn't have to go through this agony; if I'd never lived, I wouldn't fear dying."

We sound, in those moments, very much like Job: "I wish I had died in my mother's womb or died the moment I was born. Why did my mother hold me on her knees? Why did she feed me at her breast? If I had died then, I would be at rest now, sleeping like the kings and rulers who rebuilt ancient palaces" (Job 3:11-14, TEV). I'm thankful that Job is in the Bible. His story is *my* story and your story and the story of every man and every woman. For all of us there is no escape from human agony.

When it comes to human agony, the scoreboard tallies new records every single day. During the last few days, as I've been writing, two kindergarteners were killed when their yellow bus was crushed by a train; the little first grader across the street was hospitalized with what looks like leukemia (I moan, "Oh no! not again!"); a woman called to tell me how her sister, sick for

51

twenty-five years, finally died with blood flowing from her hemorrhaging eyes; a mother in tears described her sixteen-year-old son's death one wintry night six years ago while her husband standing next to me clutched his fifth drink of the evening—all this in just the last few days. All around me are the devastating accidents, the unplanned intrusion of sorrow and despair. It's everywhere. It's for every man, every woman. And as I said, the young are catching on very early these days. Maybe that's why the music is so loud, the disco beat so violent, the smoke so garishly green and orange. Maybe the young are saying, "If not this, then emptiness and death."

At some point I have to come to grips with human suffering, and Job is the book that handles this at the deepest level. ("Thank you, Lord, for leveling with me, for letting Job push the questions all the way to the doorstep of your throne room.") Sometimes I can hardly believe God let this book stay in the Bible. Why didn't He edit out such things as these?

> "When an innocent man suddenly dies, God laughs. God gave the world to the wicked. He made all the judges blind. And if God didn't do it, who did?"   (9:23,24, TEV)

> "As soon as I sin, I'm in trouble with you, but when I do right, I get no credit."   (10:15, TEV)

> "But my dispute is with God, not you; I want to argue my case with him."   (13:3, TEV)

> "God uses me for target practice and shoots arrows at me from every side—arrows that pierce and wound me and even then he shows me no pity. He wounds me again and again; he attacks like a soldier gone mad with hate."
>   (16:12-14, TEV)

> "Can't you see it is God who has done this?"   (19:6, TEV)

> "I call to you, O God, but you never answer; and when I pray, you pay no attention. You are treating me cruelly; you persecute me with all your power . . . . Why do you attack a ruined man, one who can do nothing but beg for pity?"   (30:20,21,24, TEV)

Job, of course, was wrong about some of his accusations; still, there's a realism here about the human condition, about the suffering that comes with life. Part of the realism is expressed in

Job's frank declaration that his big problem is with God.

Another important part of the realism is that the book of Job is *complete*. All the elements in the human drama are found here, those on earth and those in heaven. There is God and there is Satan. There are people, both as victims and as bystanders. Left to ourselves we'd be able only to talk about ourselves, the victims and the bystanders; through the book of Job we learn that our lives can't be explained solely in terms of God's love for us; we must take account of the enemy's presence in the world. God is active, but so is His enemy. God sets limits, but the enemy does damage all the way up to the boundaries. At Calvary Satan suffered the final defeat; since then he goes around as a wounded animal—dying, but nonetheless vicious.

A practical lesson to be learned from the book of Job is to be careful about making trite or foolish comments on human suffering. In fact a part of our suffering may be the explanations we give for it. Job, for example, suffered more than the stunning reversal from luxury to poverty, and more than the aching bones and crusty, weeping skin; Job especially suffered the stupidities his friends served up as comfort and advice. I'm sure their words were the going coin of comfort in that day, the accepted explanations for evil. The theologian Eliphaz earnestly assured the wretched sufferer that his (Eliphaz's) words had been learned from gray-haired men and were, therefore, reliable. Bildad claimed wisdom. Zophar liked to sound poetic. And then there are the long, tedious speeches of Job's youngest friend, Elihu, who—like some other young people I've known—couldn't escape the conviction that his nearness to the womb gave him a special, untarnished insight. To a person the friends agreed that since God is just, Job must be guilty of some grievous sin. So they rendered advice which is foolish, and comfort which is discomforting.

A woman once told me before she died, "I don't believe God gave me this cancer. It came from Satan." I don't remember how I responded, but I think now that she was right...and wrong. While we're in this world, we're subject to all sorts of evil and destruction which we trace to Satan. He's the origin of pain and death. And yet, there's the nagging truth that God controls everything. Our problem is with God. That's what Job said, and he wasn't wrong.

The book of Job gives an answer to that problem, and it is God's answer, not humanity's. Out of the storm God speaks to Job and reminds him that He is sovereign. Period. That's it. That's God's answer to our problem. He does not give us all His reasons (as if we could understand them anyway); He doesn't even outline a "theory of suffering." God's answer to Job's (and our) questions ultimately came to this, "I am God; I am not human. You may raise your questions and call for answers, but you will only be comforted when you believe that I am God, and I am sovereign." When Job finally confessed that God was sovereign (Job 42:2), he stopped asking other questions and regretted his own frustration ("I am ashamed of all I have said and repent in dust and ashes" 42:6, TEV).

We are taught from early childhood to seek answers which we can understand. The book of Job teaches that when we ask the ultimate question, "Why am I here and why must I suffer?" we can hardly understand the ultimate answer, "God is sovereign." With Job, we must believe it without fully understanding it.

As with Job, God gives us plenty of evidence that He is almighty, sovereign—the birds and the rivers and the mountains and trees are still there for their Maker to show us and say, "I am God." But God shows us something that Job never saw: the cross where His own Son died, and the tomb from which He rose again. Seeing that, we know God is not only sovereign, but also loving. And that's a more complete answer than we read in the final chapter of Job.

The book of Job is part of the Bible; it's only a part. The revelation of the *whole* Bible is the fact that God is loving. God is sovereign indeed, and He can and may do anything He pleases. That's good, but the sovereign God who can do all this *is* love. I need the book of Job to see suffering, but to see grace I need a clear view of Jesus.

I don't believe that Job on the ash heap could see Jesus on the cross. But I can. And I know that none of us will ever suffer as Christ suffered. Golgotha, Calvary, agony, anguish—because of that suffering, I need never go through the agony of Job. God is love—I know that now—and will always deal with me in love.

The answer to our suffering is found in God's sovereignty and

His love. Apart from that answer suicide begins to make sense. But in the shadow of Calvary it is impossible to "curse God and die." We are drawn, instead, to look up and live.

Suggested Bible Readings

Jonah is another Bible book about an angry man. Job accuses God of being cruel and arbitrary. Jonah accuses God of being kind and wishywashy. But God's answer to both shows the Sovereign Creator caring for His creatures.

Jonah 1-4; Matthew 18

CHAPTER TWELVE

Corvair in the Air

It was the craziest car I'd seen in a long time. Once it had been an ordinary Corvair, but now—with bumpers a good five feet off the road—it was truly a "Corvair in the air." When I first saw it cruising through town, I was stunned for a second or two; then I laughed out loud. Whoever had put that Corvair in the air must have been pretty stupid.

Wait a minute. The kid who did all the work would probably disagree. If I had shouted up at him while he was waiting for a traffic light, "I think your car's stupid," he probably would have parachuted down and told me how wrong I was. He might even have taken a poke at me. Anyway, I'm sure he didn't think his car was stupid at all. Somehow he had put together some good reasons to justify all the work and money he had put into his crazy Corvair. But I still think he was stupid.

Although I may seem too critical of the young man with the heavenly Corvair, I only want to show there's a strong streak of "unwisdom" in most of us, me included. The Corvair in the air represents what all of us do in one way or another. Let's face it: Some of us are unwise about cars. Some of us do some stupid things with clothes. Some of us do foolish things on the job or at school. Others of us botch up our marriage or treat our children foolishly. Like the kid with the Corvair, most of us are unwise in one way or another.

Several books in the Bible deal with matters like jacking up Corvairs and staying away from your best friend's wife and spanking your kids at appropriate times. These books, called the wisdom literature of the Bible, are Proverbs, Ecclesiastes, and Song of Solomon. That they are in the Bible at all is proof that the Christian religion is practical. Being a Christian has everything to do with day-to-day decisions we make about our cars, our clothes, our dates, our mates, and our children.

"It's possible to read the wisdom literature of the Bible as if it were simply wisdom literature and nothing more...like the wisdom literature of the Arabs. But that is a mistake...." The warning came from Bassam Madany, a friend of mine who grew up in the Middle East with proverbs from the *Koran* and other Arabic sources. I thanked him for the word of caution and resolved to remember that wisdom literature apparently had a practical meaning...but much more.

Another friend, Isaac Jen, added a different note of warning. He reminded me that proverbs can be tremendously powerful in the mind of a people. He explained how Confucius provided the Chinese people with all kinds of wise sayings which molded the Chinese mind. Not even Mao Tse-tung was able to erase Confucius's influence, said my friend Isaac. After Mao died, the Chinese people started quoting Confucius again.

To these warnings, I added my own. I knew that the Christian faith is not a faith built on hundreds of wise sayings. A Christian is a person who knows Christ, not a hundred proverbs. And even the many proverbs found in the book by that name indicate they are expressions of a certain something that is called Wisdom—Wisdom with a capital *W*. Chapter 8 of Proverbs describes Wisdom in great detail, and in the light of the entire Bible it is clear that this Wisdom is Christ Himself. The New Testament calls Jesus the person in whom are hid all the treasures of widsom and knowledge (Col. 2:3). Because we have the whole Bible, I suppose Christians tend to focus on Jesus rather than on a list of wise sayings. This is the way it ought to be.

Still, now that I know Christ, I must spend time regularly with the books He has given which contain the wisdom of God. From Proverbs I get the distinct feeling God is peeking into my private life—into how I love to sleep in, into the food I eat, into how I get along with my wife. And reading Proverbs, I *know* that God is definitely against bad sex, drunkenness, laziness, and dishonesty. Obvious? Yes, but the obvious has to be said over and over again for stupid people like me, and Proverbs says it all.

Perhaps I am using the word *stupid* too much. Please excuse me. But there's a reason: Much of the trouble men and women get themselves into—and I know about this firsthand—is not because they are mean and deliberately evil, but because they are very unwise. One of the most embarrassing things about our sin is that it is not grand. We do not sin grandly; we sin stupidly. Satan, I suppose, sins grandly. Each of his sins is part of his great plan to unseat God. But human beings sin foolishly.

The possibility of being foolish is never far from any one of us. I often pray, "Lord, keep me safe today," but maybe I should pray even more, "Lord, keep me from becoming a fool today." Foolishness in many forms runs along at our heels like a playful dog, and every once in a while nips at our legs.

The book of Proverbs helps keep me from getting bitten. God in His wisdom combats my foolishness with all these proverbs; yes, and I'm so thankful that it is with *these* proverbs. They are different from the proverbs of Confucius or of the Arabic-speaking people. In Proverbs I encounter a wisdom that flows out of my relationship with God. God rescues from our foolishness not by waking us up in the morning and making us recite ten wise sayings, but by bringing us into fellowship with Him through Jesus. He makes us His covenant children; He cautions us about the pitfalls of life; He urges us to live this day again expressing our love for Him before everything else.

It's clear from Proverbs that there is no greater pitfall, no greater stupidity than that of adultery. Again and again, the Proverbs preach that adultery is a bad trade all around. The sensuous moment, the night of pleasure on perfumed sheets, unleashes the furious passions of jealousy and poisons social relationships. Those who do not learn the self-control that confines sex to their own holy marriage destroy themselves and everything around them.

Proverbs' emphasis on sexual purity seems tailor-made for our times. Nowadays cheap, promiscuous sex drifts into our lives at every turn. Our supermarket shopping is done to the Muzak tune of "Nobody does it better." Our driving is paced by an eight-track on the dash that sings about sex all day long. Even some churches have occasionally been invaded by foolish little preachers telling their lecherous little flocks that it's okay to trade off wives and husbands. Far-fetched? Not really. My neighbor of several years ago, Pastor Hobbs, spirited his entire congregation away to another state where they practice such foolishness.

Let there be no mistake. The wisdom of God leads to purity, not to filthiness. It leads to the kind of healthy eroticism that I find in the Song of Solomon. Eroticism in the Bible? Oh, yes. The Bible does not view human sexuality as something frigid and antiseptic, something to be used only to propagate the human race. In fact, the biblical view is quite the opposite, as you know if you've read the Song of Solomon. Here is a pure eroticism that is thoroughly healthy and rewarding for both the lover and the beloved. Here is a book which shows what God intended when He created us male and female. Bad sex is as foolish as ever. Those who are truly wise with the wisdom that comes from living with Jesus know a better way.

In addition to Proverbs and the Song of Solomon, there's that strange and sometimes frustrating book called Ecclesiastes. I feel uneasy when that book is quoted to me as the last word on a subject—"There is a time to live and a time to die, a time to weep and a time to laugh, a time to embrace and a time to refrain from embracing." Beautiful? Yes. Helpful? Not really. To make sense of Ecclesiastes, I have to read it as an insight into the mind of a person who looks at the world in the light of the world alone. Only such a person could say again and again, "Vanity of vanities! All is vanity." I read Ecclesiastes as God's expose of what it must be to live without hope and without God.

The end of the matter, according to the writer of Ecclesiastes, is this: "Fear God, and keep his commandments; for this is the whole duty of man." With these words, Ecclesiastes comes back into focus and life no longer seems vain. Now the only excuse for my stupidity is my stupidity, and God has provided a remedy for that: His Son Jesus Christ and the books which teach us His wisdom.

Proverbs exposes the foolishness of too little knowledge. Ecclesiastes mourns the vanity of too much knowledge. Both teach wisdom—the fear of the Lord, the beginning and end of all right living.

Ecclesiastes 1-12; Matthew 11:1-19

CHAPTER THIRTEEN

Seventeen in Samaria

I think *Seventeen* magazine would have sold well in Samaria back around the year 760 B.C. The cows of Bashan would have liked it. *Cosmopolitan* too—there were lots of "Cosmopolitan Girls" already then.

The cows of Bashan were the pampered women in the northern kingdom whom rough-hewn Amos singled out as the culprits most responsible for the decay of their nation (Amos 4:1). I can see where they were largely to blame. Spoiled, selfish, godless, sensuous, demanding that their men give them everything they wanted, these women set the direction their society took. Give it to them, Amos:

> Listen to this, you women of Samaria, who grow fat like the well-fed cows of Bashan, who mistreat the weak, oppress the poor, and demand that your husbands keep you supplied with liquor!

Amos was out of place in Israel. He'd come from the wind-swept highlands of Tekoa where his companions had usually been scraggly-haired sheep. He must have felt ill-at-ease making his way through the cities of Israel during the reign of Jeroboam II. God had pulled him out of a lonely outpost and had given him a message of prophetic judgment against the decaying nation of Israel. Nothing in his background made him a natural candidate to be God's spokesman (7:14). But God put fire in his bones and filled his mouth with a divine message of judgment that stunned the people. Of course, they sent him back home.

Back in Tekoa, on the edge of the desert, he sat down and wrote the message he had laid on the nation of Israel. Amos was the first of the writing prophets, and the text of his message has been well preserved. It can still stun us today.

The book of Amos is a mirror which not only shows us the pampered heifers of Bashan, but reflects an image of ourselves. What's more, this mirror is truthful, not flattering. The book of Amos doesn't let us see ourselves as we would like to ("Not too bad...not too bad..."); instead it reflects all the blemishes we want to deny are really there. By listening to Amos's description of how God looked at Samaria, we can see how God looks at those of us who live in strikingly similar times.

Samaria, as Amos knew her, seemed to be enjoying a time of general confidence and prosperity, not unlike that which we enjoy in the Western World today. After years of upheaval both Judah and Israel hit a happy stride under the leadership of efficient monarchs. King Uzziah brought peace to Judah; King Jereboam II brought wealth to Israel, enriching her public and private purses with the spoils of war. Yet—listening to the cries of the oppressed—everyone in Judah and in Israel must have known that the good times wouldn't last, that all the peace and prosperity were nervously balanced on the razor edge of catastrophe. Then, as now, there was a desperate attempt on the part of many to get what they could for themselves—at the expense of the poor. "You first, after me," was as much the motto in Amos's day as it is in ours. And the cows of Bashan—painting their eyes and testing their soft couches—led the way.

It may surprise us that the cows of Bashan and their husbands, children, and friends...were regular churchgoers who wouldn't think of missing a service at Bethel or Dan or Gilgal. But God knew they practiced religion for their own amusement, that their religion was long on ceremony and short on action, that it was a perversion of the true religion revealed in Moses' writings. And God hated it! Speaking through Amos, He thundered, "I hate your religious festivals; I cannot stand them!" But the cows of Bashan went right on enjoying the good, religious life.

People enjoy religion nowadays, too, because there are many elements of religion that are very entertaining. There are religious Disney Worlds throughout North America where you go to hear great gospel music and interesting speakers. Listen to the song leader at the convention banquet: "Come now, let's all sing as loud as we can; sing it joyfully—'Jesus keep me near the cross, There a precious fountain'—c'mon, sing now...everybody!" And what minister hasn't had the cockles of his paranoid heart warmed by some sweet matron who clasps his hand warmly after a service and declares, "Pastor, I *enjoooyed* that...!"?

When times are good, people may not be all that interested in the church, but they kinda' like it when Billy Joel gets a little religious when he sings, and evangelicals smile broadly when Mormons Donnie and Marie swoon that they do believe "...everytime they hear a newborn baby cry." There's a good, foot-stomping, adrenalin-rousing quality about religion now, just as there was in Amos's time: The people of Israel went out to watch a paid prophet put on a professional show at Gilgal.

God hates religion like that. He did then, and there's no reason to think He stopped hating it when Reformed and Presbyterian churches came around. The only kind of religion God can stomach is the kind that makes human life more pure and holy and righteous and just.

And that's the second thing I learn from Amos's mirror: God is intensely interested in justice and righteousness. What's God listening for? What's He looking at? I know my religion is worth something only if I'm looking in the same direction as God, only if I'm interested in what interests Him. Amos says that if I'm wondering what interests God, I can stop wondering: He's definitely interested in righteousness and justice.

When Jeroboam II swept out with his armies, extending the borders of the land, some people got richer and richer while others got poorer and poorer. The ordinary farmers didn't do well at all. They had to fight when there was fighting to be done, and then they had to go back home and clear out the weeds that had swarmed over their fields while they were gone. The upper-class people did little fighting but got most of the booty, while the poorer people's percentage kept slipping. The rich got more and more religious while they turned their eyes away from those whose lot was becoming worse and worse. God wasn't impressed at all with the growing religion; when He looked at the land, He saw the desperate lot of the poor.

I find God's overriding interest in justice and righteousness extremely upsetting. I can easily forget all about justice, so long as I'm not being mistreated. Too many things insulate me from the plight of the disadvantaged. I am too seldom in the company of the poor. When I am, their situation is so different from mine, I have to force myself to believe they're exactly the same kind of human being that I am. Besides, it seems impossible for me to do something that could actually bring about change in their lives.

When you're comfortable and wealthy, it's easy to forget those who are miserable and poor. And forgetting is participating in the establishment of injustice and unrighteousness.

And what about the worship I enjoy? There is no doubt that *God* doesn't enjoy it so long as it is an escape from the ugly realities of our unjust world. A faithful response to Amos's book requires action among us; God calls us to express our Christian obligations as citizens...in politics, for example. I think of small groups of Christians (the Association for Public Justice, for example, or the Committee for Justice and Liberty), and I read about their insistence that Christians fight hard for justice in their nations. In religion, Jesus brings salvation; in economics, He brings equity; in politics, He brings justice. Justice—how totally interested in it our God is!

Jesus was sent to bring about a renewal of justice not merely in North America, or merely in our world, but in the universe. God is interested enough in justice and righteousness to die for it, and He did. Can you imagine, then, how He must feel when Christians sing their songs and applaud their preachers while ignoring the cries of the poor and the empty stomachs of the downtrodden?

In chapter 5 Amos reminds the people that when he talks about their sins (which are so frighteningly close to my own), he's not just making interesting conversation. He talks about a coming day of judgment when distraught sinners who once enjoyed religion would flee from one danger only to run head-on into another. These terrified sinners were not utterly evil; they were the very same people who had been having so much fun playing church. They had enjoyed the services at Dan and Bethel and Gilgal. But they'd been totally blind to the real conditions within their country; they hadn't been one bit concerned that while they were singing psalms, other people were being oppressed.

When I compare that situation to my own, I wonder if there's any hope for people like me. I'm glad that I can answer, "Yes, I think there is. There's hope because God in His good providence has arranged for Amos's blunt, fearsome message to be written down for people like me to read. Left on my own, I wouldn't have a chance of changing. But so long as I can keep my life open to the message of prophets like Amos, my life can be jolted enough to head me in the right direction."

God has kept sharp the prophet's words so that my friends and I can hear them now. Hearing them, I see Amos, sent back to Tekoa by the angry citizens of Israel, hunkering down by his sheep once more, taking up his writing materials, and putting it all down. And there's a real possibility that only after he had written it all as God wanted him to did the Spirit allow him to write the closing paragraphs which talk of God's great restoration. From a distance the prophet could see beyond the fat cows of Bashan, past the obnoxious worship of those who mouthed the psalms and kicked the poor, to the refreshing day God will "let justice roll down like waters, and righteousness like an ever-flowing stream" (5:24).

Suggested Bible Readings

Jeremiah was an unwilling prophet, a draftee. He asked to be excused. "Ah, Lord, God, I do not know how to speak, for I am only a youth...." Later he complained, "Lord, you have deceived me. I have become a laughingstock. Everyone mocks me."

Jesus was a volunteer. But that made no difference. He was treated even more crudely.

Jeremiah 1:4-12; 11:1-11,21-23; 20:1-13; 38:1-28; 39:1-14; 43:1-7; 44:11-16; Matthew 20:17-28

CHAPTER FOURTEEN

Prophet to an Age
of Madness

There are times when I think I live in an age of
pure madness. Take, for example, the time I read the following:
> Through a haze of laughing gas, pills, amyl nitrate and
> marijuana in his booth above the floor, [the disc jockey]
> adds to the body of the producer's song by beefing up the
> drum beats, accenting the bass range, emphasizing strings
> to make the dancers sway or weaving parts of records
> together to form new songs. "Drugs really make the ex-
> perience almost spiritual," he says. "A feeling of musical
> unity, of love in the room."
>
> (*Newsweek*, April 2, 1979, p. 63)

When I read that description of San Francisco's hottest disco-
theque (named, by the way, The Stud), I remember Jeremiah,
the prophet to an age of madness.

Actually, Jeremiah was only one of those ("the pre-exilic
prophets") who tried to warn the nation of impending doom.
He's in the tradition of Isaiah, who worked about a hundred
years earlier; Amos, Hosea, Micah, Nahum, and Zephaniah also
fit in here. Some of them worked furiously in Israel, but when
Jeremiah started his ministry to Jerusalem, Israel was already
whipped and many of her people had been carried off. That was,
in fact, one feature which made Jerusalem's continuing wicked-
ness incredible: Why would the citizens of Jerusalem keep sin-

ning after seeing their northern family's punishment?

Jeremiah doesn't use the term *mad* to describe his times or the people to whom he was sent. *Worthless* was his term: "They worshiped worthless idols and became worthless themselves" (2:5, TEV). The unthinkable had happened: People who'd rubbed shoulders with God, who'd been delivered and surrounded by grace, had turned away from Him to fall in love with dumb idols who couldn't tie their own shoes. God had been traded in: "My people have exchanged me," He said, ". . .for gods that can do nothing for them" (2:11, TEV). In fact, God's children had turned vicious in ways He hadn't even contemplated:

"They have built altars for Baal in order to burn their children in the fire as sacrifices. I never commanded them to do this; it never even entered my mind." (19:5, TEV)

The people of Israel had become so corrupt they didn't even know how to blush anymore (6:15).

Into that setting, Jeremiah was sent with the message, "Things are going to get worse." The Assyrians, who'd continually harassed the northern kingdom, were losing power. As Jeremiah's career opened, Babylon established itself by defeating the Egyptians at the battle of Carchemish (605 B.C.). And there, right between the major, warring nations, sat little, drunken, idol-loving Judah. Even the memory of David's mighty empire was a mockery. One of Jeremiah's tasks, in fact, involved convincing the people that those days were over—that Judah had to give in to the Chaldeans, to Babylon.

But the earthy, political arena is only the setting of Jeremiah —it isn't the whole story. Much of this book demonstrates how close God is to His people, how involved God is in our affairs. When I read Jeremiah, I get the distinct impression that the prophet represents God not only in terms of the message he speaks, but even in terms of the way he feels. When we peer into the prophet's soul, I believe we're looking into the heart of God. The seething frustration with human corruption, the quiet agony of losing one's children—the emotions reflected in Jeremiah are, I think, the emotions of God Himself.

That's not to deny that the book is about Jeremiah; of course, it is. He was God's special messenger, a man marked for absolute contrast to those around him. The pathetic prophet was segregated away, commanded not to marry, denied the privilege of a family, instructed not to join the people even in their mourning. His message was so dismal, so sure to lead to his persecution, that he hated to announce it. While there's genuine divine presence here, there's also real human drama. Jeremiah was warmhearted and sympathetic, yearning for human acceptance. No wonder he wanted to be released from his calling, to "forget the Lord and no longer speak in his name." But that was when Jeremiah knew most certainly that he'd been captured by God: "Then your message is like a fire burning deep within me. I try my best to hold it in, but can no longer keep it back" (20:9, TEV).

And all of this is set in the worst of times, one of those chaotic hours of history when wisdom is evicted and foolishness reigns supreme, when stupidities become the rule rather than the exception, when all who represent truth and justice—even God Himself—are universally despised.

Parallels can be drawn between our times and Jeremiah's: Sensitivity to sin rarely produces blushes these days either, and truth and justice are no more popular today than ever. The power struggle between major nations isn't gone—only the names have changed. Today we have China, Russia, and the United States, instead of Egypt, Assyria, and Chaldea.

These similarities are overwhelmingly depressing unless we also see the greatest parallel between our day and Jeremiah's. In spite of all the gloomy things to be said about Jeremiah's times, the overriding message coming from his book is one of hope. Jeremiah, you see, was not a pessimist; he was a prophet. Rising above the madness of his age, the flexing muscle of Babylon, the soldier's shield, and the prophet's pen, Jeremiah saw the *covenant of God*. What he saw then, we can see now. That is the greatest parallel between Jeremiah's audience and mine.

Tennessee Williams has a play whose plot involves a farmer who kept a herd of donkeys in a corral. One morning the farmer discovered the donkeys were gone—and getting them back proved nearly impossible. According to Williams, that's a picture of God's relation to the world. Things appear to have gotten somewhat out of hand, and God is busy full-time trying to "get back the donkeys." The playwright's point is the same as the prophet's: When God's people break their covenant and go running off, God keeps the covenant by going after them. From the human side, the covenant is shattered; from the side of God, it's shatterproof. It was in Jeremiah's day, and it still is today.

So, during those same depressing moments when Jeremiah was promising Jerusalem captivity and slavery, he also turns on the light of the covenant: "I will maintain my covenant with Jacob's descendants and with my servant David. . . .I will be merciful to my people and make them prosperous again" (33:26, TEV). So faithful is God that when the old covenant is ruined, violated by our sin, He simply surprises us again: "The time is coming when I will make a new covenant with the people of Israel and with the people of Judah. . . .I will put my law within them and write it on their hearts. I will be their God, and they will be my people. . . .I will forgive their sins and I will no longer remember their wrongs" (31:31-34, TEV).

On Calvary the new covenant was delivered; at Pentecost God's law was written on human hearts. And since the day of Jeremiah forgiveness has always and only come by God's grace. Jeremiah pinned all hope for his age of madness on that covenant of grace, and in our present age—marked by drugs, discotheques, and depravity—it's still the only hope we have.

But it's also the only hope we need.

Suggested Bible Readings
Queen Esther risked her life to save her people. King Jesus did far more. Yet while Esther is still honored by a yearly festival, Jesus is not yet recognized as "King of the Jews."

Esther; John 19:1-22

CHAPTER FIFTEEN

Prisoners of War

He had a peculiar name, both first and last, and both had been given to his son. When I asked why he'd passed on that name, there was a long pause before he responded:

> My wife was pregnant when the army shipped me overseas. Before I left, we agreed our children wouldn't be named after relatives, not even ourselves. But by the time the baby was born, I was listed as missing in action. My wife assumed I was dead. In fact, I was in a prison camp...

His words trailed off as if he'd lost the point of his story...but then he looked up and quickly finished:

> By the time I met my son, we had the same name. It was the only thing of mine my wife could give our child.

The prison experience, whether it's in the county jail or a concentration camp, breaks every pattern in human life. Husbands and wives are separated. Parents and children become strangers. Despair so piercing and lonesome that it can hardly be described settles into the gray cell with the slouching prisoner.

Throughout the centuries, in nearly all cultures, writing has provided a means of release for those who have no other freedoms left. When Solzhenitsyn wrote One Day in the Life of Ivan Denesovich, he already believed that a man is never more free than when he's a prisoner. Martin Luther King's "Letter from a Birmingham Prison..." spoke eloquently of the injustices which led him to jail. Letters from Prison by Dietrich

Bonhoeffer, *Out of the Night* by Jan Valtin, *Soul on Ice* by Eldridge Cleaver, *The Hiding Place* by Corrie Ten Boom—all are illustrations of literature known as "prison writing."

The Bible contains prison writing too. Some of Paul's New Testament letters are well-known examples. But the Old Testamemt books of Ezekiel, Daniel, and Esther also fit that category: They describe Israel in exile, an imprisoned nation.

For the people of Israel the exile was a horrible but cleansing process that flushed idolatry out of their souls and away from their nation. With unusual flair, and even high drama, Ezekiel brought God's fierce word to the people:

> "The city of murders is doomed! I myself will pile up the firewood. Bring more wood! Fan the flames! Cook the meat! Boil away the broth! Burn up the bones!... Jerusalem, your immoral actions have defiled you. Although I tried to purify you, you remained defiled. You will not be pure again until you have felt the full force of my anger. I, the Lord, have spoken. The time has come for me to act. I will not ignore your sins or show pity or be merciful. You will be punished for what you have done."
>
> (Ezek. 24:9-14, TEV)

The tragedy of captivity was increased because it came in waves spread over twenty years (from 605-586 B.C.), rather than in a single campaign from which the people could recover. Each time Judah's kings failed to heed Jeremiah's warning not to rebel against Babylon, raiders came and dragged more captives off to Babylon. Among the first to go were Daniel and Ezekiel who became prison prophets, inmate chaplains for a captive people.

For Daniel the exile was a time of maturing. As a fourteen-year-old boy he was the first to decline the king's food in that distant land, thereby risking his life for the truth he'd learned as a child. When the captivity came to an end, and the lives of the Jews had been spared, an aged Daniel watched the people stream back to their homeland.

For Ezekiel the exile was a time of prophecy. No less dramatic than Jeremiah, Ezekiel made a public spectacle of himself when acting out the siege of Jerusalem (Ezek. 4) and playing the part of a refugee (Ezek. 12). But he was also intensely human; in a moving moment we see him forcing back his tears, sobbing privately at the death of his wife (Ezek. 24).

And then there is Esther, whose story is a curious mixture of oriental intrigue and covenant history. It's a story which contains everything needed to make a "rags-to-riches," X-rated movie: A young Jewish girl, born in captivity, made a candidate for the king's harem, selected for her beauty by a lustful, heathen king—and in the background, the politician Haman schemes against the heroine's uncle Mordecai who counters with shrewd moves of his own.

Taken out of the biblical context and dropped into a Hollywood studio the story of Esther could become a box-office hit. Taken *in* its biblical context, Esther is a powerful testimony to the gentle grace with which God nursed His children even while they were being disciplined in exile. That confession is neatly summarized when Mordecai reminds his frightened niece:

> "If you keep quiet at a time like this, help will come from heaven to the Jews, and they will be saved, but you will die and your father's family will come to an end. Yet who knows—maybe it was for a time like this that you were made queen!" (Esther 4:14, TEV)

This brief period of exile was crucial for Judah. It was in the exile, when the people of God sat and wept, reluctant to sing their songs for taunting enemies (Ps. 137), that many of them first saw the truth about their own idolatry. They began to value, and even collect, the word of God which they had previously abused. Dr. Jack Scott claims:

> In these days of exile and return, the Jews became, even away from Jerusalem, a religious community. There was an increasing interest in the study of the Jewish Scriptures....Synagogues arose both in exile and in Judah wherever there were Jewish believers.*

In addition to providing Judah with a badly needed purging, the exile also left an impressive impact on the captor, Babylon. God's sinning people were drawn into the central city in the world. There, as prisoners, they found revival. And in their revival, the pagan city itself was thoroughly shaken. Babylon's favorite god, Marduk, was unseated from his throne. Who could

*Jack B. Scott, *God's Plan Unfolded* (Wheaton, Illinois: Tyndale House Publishers, 1976), p. 293.

stay loyal to Marduk when the God of Abraham, Isaac, and Jacob pinched shut the mouths of hungry lions and cooled the flames of an angry furnace? Hundreds of years before Paul and Barnabas sang out in prison and began converting jailers, the captive Israel made its mark in the center of a hostile world. As Jeremiah had confidently predicted, "Babylon has fallen! Her god Marduk has been shattered! Babylon's idols are put to shame; her disgusting images are crushed!" (Jer. 50:2, TEV).

In the books of Daniel, Ezekiel, and Esther we see that the sordid history of God's disobedient children is used by the Almighty to build a new creation. We can not account for the harsh punishment of exile simply by noting Israel's sin; we must also look beyond the exile and see that it was one means by which God brought His grace.

There came a day when wise men, descendants of those who had tormented Israel in her captivity, followed a star and worshiped an infant. Their ancestors had crushed Jerusalem and defiled the temple of the Jews. Now the wise men crossed a desert toward Jerusalem where the temple had been rebuilt, and there they knelt before (who would have believed it?) the King of the Jews. In that moment of worship the children of Babylon bowed before the God of Israel as they had never done before.

In the end the story of Israel's exile is really the story of God's redemption. The people entered freedom with a grace they had discovered during their exile. And the lesson was not only for one nation or one people. In the Babylonian revival of Israel, which spread to Babylon itself, we see that God had something much grander than captivity in mind. He had His eye already fixed on a stable in Bethlehem and a cross on the edge of Jerusalem. Already you could hear the words, "For God so loved the *world...*" (John 3:16)!

Suggested Bible Readings

The returning exiles had trouble with the Samaritans. The trouble grew partly out of religious and political differences and partly out of Samaritan outrage at Jewish exclusiveness. Bad feeling between the two groups was still strong in Jesus' day. But Jesus overcame it with a new inclusiveness of spirit and truth.

Nehemiah 1; 2; 4-7:4; 8; 9; John 4:1-42

CHAPTER SIXTEEN

The Wet Congregation and the Gloomy Bartender

One of my major faults is that I tend to think of Christianity as a minor force in the world. So much seems bigger: General Motors, for instance, and the United Nations, or the Canadian Broadcasting Corporation (CBC). My religion, on the other hand, is private, involving my personal relationship with God and a meeting every seventh day with other people who believe as I do. I'm inclined to view my faith and the faith of my fathers as of little consequence in the great affairs of human history.

When I realize I'm thinking this way, I'm always ashamed of myself. The Bible flatly contradicts such a narrow description of the Christian faith. Jesus' statement just before He ascended, "All authority in heaven and on earth has been given to me" (Matt. 28:18), comes as no surprise. Since Adam and Eve's exit from the garden, the whole Old Testament points toward this conclusion. The God of Abraham, Isaac, and Jacob is always described as the God of earth, sea, and sky. World affairs are in the hands of Israel's God, and He has no difficulty controlling the history of His creation. That becomes crystal clear in the stories of the wet congregation and the gloomy bartender.

The story of the wet congregation involves the assembly of people who came together in the rain to hear their great leader Ezra call them to renewal. Lives needed to be purified; marriages needed to be cleansed. The people of Israel needed to change their ways dramatically, to demonstrate that they were indeed the people of God.

The call to repentance is seldom popular, even in modern churches with well-padded pews. But how would you like to stand in the driving rain listening to someone recite a list of your sins, telling you to get rid of your marriage partner, inviting you to repent? That was the scene in Jerusalem. The congregation of people, drenched in the downpour, cried out for mercy. In a sense, it was the only reasonable thing to do. I can imagine someone calling out from the crowd, "Look, this is crazy! The crowd is huge and it's raining hard. Our sin is great and needs some lengthy attention. Just let us go home, will you, Ezra? The officials can stay in Jerusalem and work out the matter. Then you can let us know, and we'll happily straighten out our lives." (See Ezra 10:12 ff.)

Okay, the conditions were rough—but the confession extracted from the wet congregation was genuine enough. These were the people who had returned to Jerusalem from exile in Babylon; some of them had helped in rebuilding God's temple. As they stood there in the rain renewing their covenant with God, they remembered all the great changes God had led them through during the past century.

The Persian ruler Cyrus had destroyed the Babylonian Empire, making possible the return of God's people from the land of their imprisonment. The Babylonians had a policy of deporting people they captured and bringing them to Babylon. But the Persians had a different policy. And when Cyrus became emperor, he issued the decree that became the legal charter for the Jewish people's return to their homeland. Just as Isaiah had prophesied (Isa. 44:26-28; 45:1-13), Cyrus, the obedient servant of Almighty God, drew up the document and arranged for the return of the temple utensils. And thousands of years later we can still read the sheets torn from their log book to see the family names of all the clans who returned (Ezra 2, Neh.7).

The return, though, was not an event that occupied a few brief months. Like the exile itself, the homecoming stretched over many years in the nation's life. The first group to respond to Cyrus's decree were led by Sheshbazzar (Zerubbabel) and included many priests; those who went concentrated on rebuilding the temple. The return under Ezra didn't occur until eighty years later. During that eighty year period the whole drama we know as Esther's story unfolded. In fact, God used Esther to make possible the great work of Ezra and Nehemiah. If she had not been successful, it seems that the first group of Jews who returned to the promised land would have been swallowed up in the paganism that had overgrown the country, while the rest of the Jews would have been slaughtered in captivity.

In all of this it's clear that the people of God get top priority in the affairs of human history as God involves Himself with people. That truth is just as clear in the story of the gloomy bartender, Nehemiah.

I was recently talking with a Christian mother who was grieving because her son had taken a job in the liquor business. We both shook our heads, looked at each other soberly, and agreed that this was terrible. A few days later I was reading about Nehemiah. Suddenly it struck me: Look, Nehemiah was in the liquor business too. He was a "purveyor of alcoholic beverages." I was tempted to rush into the woman's office and announce, "Don't worry about your son. One of the most important people in the Old Testament was a bartender." But I didn't. Nehemiah was right where God wanted him, and I'm not at all certain the same could be said of her son.

One day Nehemiah brought wine in to Artaxerxes (emperor of Persia, Esther's stepgrandson), and the emperor noticed that his wine steward was depressed. That's where the story of the gloomy bartender begins. Zerubbabel had led the first return to Israel. Another had come under Ezra, about eighty years later. Now there was to be a third, led by the wine steward Nehemiah.

Nehemiah had received a dismal message from Jerusalem: The work of restoration had run aground. Part of the city's wall stood unfinished, and fire had destroyed some of the work which had been completed. In addition, the people were constantly being harassed by their enemies. The reason *Nehemiah* received this message was that, among the Jews, his rank was nearly as high as Esther's had been. Esther had gone to bed with the emperor—she was his queen. But the wine steward was with the emperor even more than the queen was; he served as the emperor's confidant.

To make the gloomy bartender's story brief, he was released from his duties and allowed to return to Jerusalem. The book which bears his name is the record of restoration under this sensitive and noble man. A priest by office, Nehemiah demonstrated enormous skill, wisdom, and efficiency in setting the people back to work. Under his direction, the walls of Jerusalem were eventually completed, and the God of the covenant was worshiped once again.

Now all of this—as I said earlier—indicates how God controls the history of our world. The welfare of God's people is always guarded by the Most High. Covenant promises made to Abraham, repeated to Abraham's offspring, seemed worthless when succeeding world powers swept over "the land of promise" and carried both the northern and the southern kingdoms away. As wave after wave of deportees were carried from their homeland, first to Nineveh and later to Babylon, the word of God spoken to Abraham seemed no differnt from the word of man: It looked weak as water.

But the God of promise, the God of covenant, was not idly watching developments meander across the plain of history. "The Lord controls the mind of a king as easily as he directs the course of a stream" (Prov. 21:1, TEV), and every one of the great rulers—Nebuchadnezzar, Cyrus, Darius, Xerxes, Artaxerxes—became God's men, accomplishing His purposes whether they meant to or not.

Seeing all this I remember again how important the Christian faith really is. Christianity is *the* world religion. All events in world history, including those in tonight's newspaper, will further the cause of Christ whether it seems that way or not. And God not only arranges the massive world events to make His covenant people prosper, but also preserves faith within His people.

In the last chapter, I said the people of Israel were purified by their exile. Cut off from the external temple, they created a synagogue in the land of their captivity; and like Ezra many of them developed new understanding of God's law. Despite the cruelties that accompanied the exile and its aftermath, God's people developed a splendid interest in His revelation. Their growth made the exile a period of heroic spiritual achievement.

Ezra's announcement of reform, spoken to a drenched congregation, could only come from a powerful conviction that God willed a renewal. Nehemiah's shrewd planning, his selfless devotion to rebuilding the city, and his commitment to continuous prayer are utterly impressive. God had obviously worked a great miracle of grace, five to six hundred miles east of the promised land, in a time of exile for His people.

When I remember that all these things happened before Christ had completed His final great work, before the promised Holy Spirit had been given, I know Christianity is no minor force in the world. The world belongs to Christ and so do we. We are called by Him, therefore, to be at least as bold and faithful as Ezra, Nehemiah, and the unknown Israelites who faithfully stood in the rain, followed a bartender, and trusted God's promises.

Suggested Bible Readings

Zerubbabel and Jeshua restored the temple; Ezra restored the law; Nehemiah restored the walls of Jerusalem. Of the three, Ezra's restoration lasted. The Torah remained through Jesus' day to the present as the living (but unfulfilled) foundation of the Jewish faith.

Ezra; Matthew 5:17-48

CHAPTER SEVENTEEN

The Liberated Wailing Wall

TuvyaZaretskyStuartDauermannBenyomin-
EllegantNaomiDauermannJimWarnockKreshaRichman-
ShoshanaMooreAvnerBoskeyJh'AnMoskowitzMarthaRuth-
BricknerIrvingKuglerLynRosen-Bond. . . .

Their names are strung end to end without punctuation, forming a border which frames lyrics from one of their albums, "We
Were Like Dreamers." They are The Liberated Wailing Wall, a
modern singing group made up of Christian Jews. The title song
from this album recaptures the exciting, frustrating, near boister-
ous time of Israel's return to the promised land. With muscular
rhythms and typically Jewish harmony, Stuart Dauermann sings
a version of Psalm 126:

> When the Lord brought back the captive ones
>   of Zion,
> We were like those who dream.
> Then our mouth was filled with laughter,
> And our tongues with joyful shouting,
> When the Lord brought the captives home.
>
> Then they said among the nations of the world
> "The Lord has done great things for them."
> Yes. You've done great things for us, Lord,
> Therefore we are glad.*

---

*Stuart Dauermann, " 'We Were Like Dreamers' (Psalm 126)" (San
Rafael, California: Jews for Jesus, 1976).

When you put the words of Psalm 126 into the mouths of return-ing exiles, it seems that the whole nation was having a spiritual high. "How we laughed, how we sang for joy!"—there's a "Hallelujah! Praise the Lord!" quality about those feelings.

What a contrast between that spiritual high and the moods of the prophets who actually worked day-by-day with those very same people. While the nation got high, the prophets chugged along, calling for obedience and reform. Things have not, I sup-pose, changed so very much. Our day-by-day performance also falls disappointingly short of the ideas which fill our hymns.

The return of the Israelites from Babylon marked a new era in Israel's history. And with that new beginning, the Old Testa-ment comes to an end. Haggai, Zechariah, Malachi...whew! I remember being asked (it seems like centuries ago) to recite the books of the Bible. The Old Testament books were always the hardest, and finally whipping through the last three was like sliding into home plate inches ahead of the throw. With these books, it's over; the sheer mass of what we've covered is im-pressive. I'm very, very eager to turn just one more page and start the New Testament which is now tantalizingly close. But if we're to fully understand the New Testament gospel, we need to read the prophecies heard by the returning exiles.

While reading these three books of prophecy, I notice that the Old Testament ends not far from where it began—human beings are still embarrassingly given to sinful failure. In Genesis we saw the fall; in Haggai, Zechariah, and Malachi we see the fallen. In all the intervening years absolutely nothing happened to in-dicate that people can save themselves. Salvation will take a divine Savior.

Haggai, Zechariah, and Malachi prophesy to a people who were seriously blemished by sin: The priesthood was not faithful (Mal. 2). The people became self-centered, neglecting the prom-ises they'd made while standing in the rain with Ezra. The un-finished temple stood as an accusation against them, a people so busy with their own projects they had no time for God's.

Because of the people's sin, the prophets' messages contain elements of threat and frightening descriptions of coming judgment—especially the prophetic warning that Jerusalem would be destroyed again. But woven through it all is this message of hope: The covenant promises God made to Abraham will surely carry the day. God will do what He purposed, and He will do it with His people. But by the time it's over and the final trumpet has sounded, God's people will include all the nations of the world.

To Haggai, the disappointing quality of the new temple becomes the signpost pointing forward to an even newer and completed temple. He reveals that one day God's temple will have a splendor that cannot be avoided—all the nations will bring their treasures there. That vision in Haggai 2, at the end of the Old Testament, is seen again in Revelation 21, at the end of the New.

Zechariah tells of "that day." It will be a day of joyous welcome for Jerusalem's king, the "king over all the earth." It will also be a birth, Zechariah described Jesus' triumphal entry (Zech. 9:9,10) and Judas's thirty pieces of silver (Zech. 11:12,13). He also presents a vision which anticipates the age of the Spirit: "You will succeed, not by military might or by your own strength, but by my spirit. . . . You will rebuild the Temple, and as you put the last stone in place, the people will shout, 'Beautiful, beautiful!' " (Zech. 4:6,7, TEV). It's all here—Pentecost, the church, and Ephesians 2:18,19.

The Old Testament closes with a promise of victory for all who will obey the Lord. In a final word on the covenant—final, that is, until Jesus—the Lord binds Himself to His people and calls them to obedient service.

The shape of faith is always obedience. It was so in Eden and at Sinai and on Calvary. It was so when Malachi wrote his prophecy, and it was still so when Paul sent letters to the New Testament churches. Though the Bible strenuously attacks any idea of salvation based on human works, the Bible also declares that faith without works is dead. From beginning to end, the consistent theme that God's people had to hear was obey, obey, obey. If that wasn't clear to the readers of Malachi, it became brutally clear to the readers of Matthew.

But that's a story yet to be told.

Zechariah tells of "that day." It will be a day of joyous welcome for Jerusalem's king, the "king over all the earth." It will also be a day when "there shall no longer be a trader in the house of the Lord of hosts." Matthew's account interweaves these.

Zechariah 7-14; Matthew 21:1-17

CHAPTER EIGHTEEN

Oh, Susanna!

Susanna was very beautiful.

"When the people went away at noon, Susanna used to go and walk in her husband's garden. Every day the two elders saw her entering the garden and taking her walk, and they were obsessed with lust for her. They no longer prayed to God, but let their thoughts stray from him and forgot the claims of morality. They were both infatuated with her; but they did not tell each other what pangs they suffered, because they were ashamed to confess that they wanted to seduce her. Day after day they watched eagerly to see her.

"One day they said, 'Let us go home; it is time for lunch.' So they went off in different directions, but soon retraced their steps and found themselves face to face. When they questioned one another, each confessed his passion. Then they agreed on a time when they might find her alone" (*Daniel and Susanna*, vs. 7-12, NEB Apocrypha).

I first discovered Daniel and Susanna many years ago when my father was the janitor of a country church outside Grand Rapids, Michigan. Occasionally I'd have to be in the church alone (say, to heat it up for an evening service), and during the long hours I'd sometimes idly leaf through the massive pulpit Bible. It was huge, old-fashioned, loaded with illustrations, and heavy as lead. It was a mountain of a book, and I thought there was none other like it.

I was surprised one day when I stumbled across several books with strange sounding names in the middle of that special Bible. There they were, printed and bound just like the rest of the books, but I'd never hear of any of them before. I was, of course, scanning the Apocrypha—though I didn't know it then—when I happened on the story of *Daniel and Susanna*. The Daniel I knew had never been like this! I read the entire book. It was short. And my, it was worth the effort.

This fascinating drama featuring two dirty old peeping toms lifting up their eyes in unholy anticipation, only to stare into each other's pupils, is typical of the Apocrypha. Another dramatic book, *Judith*, tells of a courageous and beautiful woman who lured an Assyrian general, Holophernes, into a trap where she promptly decapitated him. And *Tobit* is full of fantastical, sometimes humorous, adventures. *Daniel and Susanna*, *Judith*, *Tobit*, and other apocryphal books like them give intriguing insights into the mind of Israel during her captivity and return.

But not all apocryphal books deal with the drama and adventure of day-to-day living. Some are more philosophical, taking up intricate mysteries of the universe and human destiny. The puzzling relationship between divine sovereignty and human freedom, for example, is examined by the man (or woman) who wrote *II Esdras* (8:56).

Actually, there's little possibility that the author of *II Esdras* was a woman. Women, I'm afraid, didn't enjoy much esteem during the time the Apocrypha were written. As *Ecclesiasticus* 25:24-26 puts it:

> Woman is the origin of sin, and it is through her that we all die. Do not leave a leaky cistern to drip or allow a bad wife to say what she likes. If she does not accept your control, divorce her and send her away.

The Apocrypha portrays women as subtle and devious; even the expansion of the book of Esther makes the queen more beguiling than does the biblical account. Women here are a strange force that sets otherwise pious elders to crouching in bushes, and makes fools out of kings (*I Esdras* 4:27-33). They couldn't possibly write a book worth reading.

However, there's a soaring majesty to some books in the Apocrypha. There are few sentences anywhere that better describe our eternal hope than this from *II Esdras*: "The greatest joy of all will be the confident and exultant assurance which will be theirs, free from all fear and shame, as they press forward to see face to face the One whom they served in their lifetime, and from whom they are now to receive their reward in glory" (7:98).

Much in *Esdras* and *Ecclesiasticus* sounds biblical. Lines can be drawn between sections of these books and ideas developed further in the Bible. *Ecclesiasticus* 5:4-6, for example, carries the same idea as the sixth chapter of Romans. And the great book of *I Maccabees* tells a stirring tale of military courage and Jewish piety: Judas Maccabaeus leads a revolt against the empire. Success is remote, but the faithful Jew meticulously adheres to the laws of warfare set down in Deuteronomy 20. He leads in prayer and fasting. And then, despite the terrible military odds, he sends home first all the newly married, then all those who'd built houses and planted vineyards, and finally those who are frightened. The general knew God would give the victory (*Maccabees* 3:55-60), and He did.

The unfamiliar books taking up space in that mammoth pulpit Bible into which I looked many years ago are important. The Belgic Confession suggests that we can profit from reading them, and it's my conviction that the Confession is right—though I'd still recommend some caution. The Apocrypha is, after all, folk literature, and folk literature—like folk songs—shows the character of a people. Through the Apocrypha, we can see the character of Israel which emerged between the return from Babylon and the coming of the Savior.

The Apocrypha are also valuable in a negative way. Reading them helps us appreciate the superiority of the authentic books of Scripture. There's a noticeable difference between the book of Esther in the Old Testament and the apocryphal book of *Esther*. Similarly, there are differences between Daniel and *Daniel and Susanna*, between the biblical book of Jeremiah and the apocryphal letter that bears his name. The books in the apocryphal library are markedly inferior to the canonical books.

This contrast serves to fortify the position of the Bible books. In fact, the way the Apocrypha were handled throughout history throws useful light on the process by which the canon (the body of sixty-six accepted books) was established.

The Hebrew canon of the Old Testament never included the

apocryphal books. It was a Greek translation, the Septuagint, which first inserted Apocrypha books at various places in the Bible where they seemed to fit in. Later St. Jerome also included them in the Latin (Vulgate) Scriptures, but he made a careful distinction between them and the true Scriptures. Over the next thousand years Jerome's distinction faded and these books were mingled with the Bible itself. Finally, after the Reformation, the Roman Catholic Church's Council of Trent put these books into the canon in defiance of the Reformers who rejected them.

Some of the doctrinal differences between the Roman Catholic and Reformed churches result from just this distinction. Purgatory and prayers for the dead are commonly accepted within Roman Catholicism because both are taught in the Apocrypha. Since neither are taught in the Bible itself, the Reformed churches have never accepted them.

In the four centuries between the last Old Testament prophet and the coming of Christ, more happened than the writing of some Apocrypha. During this "intertestamentary period" the conditions developed which existed in Jesus' world, both in the Jewish nation and in the Jewish religion.

The Jews spent many of these years in bondage. After Babylon, they were slaves to the Greeks, then to the Ptolemies, then to the Seleucids, and finally to the Romans. But there was also one glorious period of independence when the Maccabees revolted and won. In a world dominated by major powers, the Maccabeans had given the Jewish people a nation with its own status from 166 to 63 B.C. The memory of this brave, independent period fired a fierce patriotism among the Jews of Jesus' day.

The Jewish religion also changed during these four hundred years. It was thoroughly fractured into a variety of sects, among them the Herodians, Sadducees, and Pharisees. Each sect found its own way to abuse historic Judaism and develop new teachings. The Pharisees, for example, developed the *Talmud*—a book of intricate laws and legal interpretations governing practically every activity of life—and the *Talmud* became more important than the Word given by God.

The Jewish nation to which Jesus came then was not the nation that had been so splendidly purified by the chastisement of the exile. And when Jesus was finally crucified, it was at the urging of people who had perverted the faith of the Old Testament so completely that the Messiah Himself became an unwelcome intruder. It was then, in the fullness of time, that "a decree went out from Caesar Augustus that all the world should be enrolled" (Luke 2:1), and the greatest chapter of history began to unfold.

Suggested Bible Readings

Susanna and Judith are brave and pure. One fights for her virtue, the other for her people. Both are heroines. Jesus' friends Mary and Martha are less heroic, but in their own way even more remarkable women.

Daniel and Susanna; Judith; John 11:1-44, 12:1-8

CHAPTER NINETEEN

The Apostolic Quartet

The *Alexandria Quartet* has never sung a song. It's a set of four books in which Lawrence Durrell explores the lives of four people living in the sun-drenched Middle East during the late 1950s. Each book is named for a major character—*Justine*, *Balthazar*, *Mountolive*, and *Clea*—and each looks at the same segment of history. What impresses the reader is how widely the descriptions of that same bit of history vary—as widely as the characters describing it.

Matthew, Mark, Luke, and John also look at one segment of history from four different perspectives. All four writers focus on Jesus. But, because each stands at a slightly different angle, each sees the Christ in a special way. Like four strong voices blending into harmony, the Gospel accounts give a full view of Jesus' life, death, and resurrection. Remove anything from any one of the Gospels, and important notes will be missing. Yet what impresses the reader is how obviously these four writers are describing *one* history.

From the very dawn of the church, people have agreed this is no ordinary quartet of writings set down by mere mortals. This is an *apostolic* quartet, a blend of writings based on eyewitness accounts of those who lived with Jesus. It was the apostles to whom Christ said, "As the Father has sent me, even so I send you" (John 20:21). It was the apostles who were uniquely equipped to remember accurately all that Jesus said and did (John 14:26). And the apostles themselves were trained by

Christ, so these four Gospels were directed by His Spirit. Over the past two thousand years the opening books of the New Testament have, more than any other writings, altered the course of human history.

In the Christian religion everything depends on the four Gospels. If Matthew, Mark, Luke, and John have lied to us about *anything*, then *none* of their testimony can be trusted. If they have perjured themselves while testifying about Jesus' miracles, for example, they may also have lied about the resurrection. Ultimately it is not the Gospels on which we must pass judgment; we must decide, rather, about the person Jesus whom we meet here. If we believe the Gospel writers are good witnesses, then we will judge that this Jesus is the Christ, the Son of the living God. The other possibility is that we will turn away, concluding that the apostolic quartet is a liars' club and Jesus is little more than one more character in a long and tortured history of the Jews. I trust the testimony of Matthew and the other three and hope you do too.

Not only our faith but our whole understanding of the Bible is built on the Gospels. If once we read (and believe) the Gospels, the entire Old Testament takes on a new complexion. We see that between Genesis ("you shall bruise his heel") and John ("for God so loved the world") the whole Old Testament is sloped toward a stable in Bethlehem where the Son of David was finally born. And if there were no Gospels, there would be no New Testament at all. We read the other sixty-two books of the Bible very differently because of these four.

Of course, all this is "old hat" to many of us who've been raised with the Gospels. It would be hard to be surprised by any of these books. But think of it: Even though we have no first century newspapers and no photographs of Jesus with His disciples, and even though the secular historians of His day didn't consider Jesus worth describing—we still have an astonishing collection of detailed writing looking at Jesus' life from four angles. Even though Jesus lived nineteen centuries ago, we can still see Him when we turn to the opening pages of the New Testament. Because of the Gospels, we can know Jesus. When I think about that, it surprises me.

But some people aren't surprised by the Gospels—and they

aren't persuaded by them either. Some readers argue that because the Gospels were written some time after Christ's life (thirty years later for the first three, probably more than that for John), they don't present biography. These critics say that many so-called "facts" presented in the Gospels are fantastic, purely imaginary, the creations of the early church. Such people think the Gospels are interesting, but not inspired—certainly nothing to stake your life on.

But recently there has been a growing recognition that the Gospels do contain historical, even biographical facts. Archeologists and historians, both Christian and non-Christian, have increasingly uncovered material which confirms the Gospel accounts. Even the Gospel of John, long thought to be the least "historical" of the Gospels, is being validated by other evidence. As Herman Ridderbos has pointed out, it's simply wrong to think the early church created the Gospels. Just the opposite is true: The gospel message shaped the early church. And every martyr for the cause of Christ since that day has staked his or her life on the truth of these accounts.

Together the Gospels are the written apostolic teaching concerning the Lord Jesus Christ. But each of the Gospels is carefully edited, and each reflects a very special point of view.

The apostle John, for example, says he wrote to convince people "that Jesus is the Christ, the Son of God, and that believing you may have life in his name" (John 20:31). This principle governed his selection of materials. When you read John's Gospel, you soon detect his pattern: Over and over again, he presses the claim that Jesus is God's Son and our Redeemer.

Or look at the Gospel Matthew wrote especially for Jewish readers. Careful students have detected that Matthew uses the numerical value of the word David (in Hebrew, David's name represents the number fourteen) in his neatly arranged genealogy of Jesus (Matt. 1). Some of Jesus' ancestors are listed; some aren't. Matthew arranged the genealogy using the number fourteen to show that Jesus is the great Son of David, the promised Messiah of Israel. In fact, throughout his gospel, Matthew assembled his material carefully, obviously conscious of the number of sentences he was devoting to each subject.

It's worth noting that the Gospels were written with great

care. Sometimes people seem to think the Holy Spirit works best when we think least. I've heard people criticize ministers for preparing sermons ahead of time; they want their preachers to be "moved by the Holy Spirit then and there" when they first stand up to preach. Previous study for the message, let alone writing out the whole sermon, is wrong—the Holy Spirit can't work that way. Well, the Holy Spirit can work that way and regularly does. And four of the clearest examples I know are the Gospels of Matthew, Mark, Luke, and John.

The Gospels teach us that this planet has been visited by the God who created the universe. We have an accurate record of the Visitor. We can observe what He did, and we can learn from His teaching. As the Old Testament begins with God walking in His garden, the New Testament opens with God coming again to redeem His whole creation. The New Testament is familiar territory to those who have come through the Old. The covenant relationship is here, now concentrated in the Lord Jesus Christ. Those who come to the Messenger of the Covenant, Jesus, will hear Him tell of the kingdom of God which comes by obedience—this is no new theme to those who've heard the prophets. What's new here is the cross, where obedience was finally maintained and the covenant was permanently sealed.

When I read the Gospels, I can be startled, exhilarated at how near these words can bring me to the life of Christ. But there's also something humbling about the fact that I should be so dependent on a book, on this book. When it comes to religion, we prefer to let our imaginations soar. When it comes to God, each of us likes to think he or she can say something as insightful as the next person. But true religion is rooted in something outside ourselves, something very narrow and definite: the Bible. In fact, it's rooted in the material taught by the apostles. To be sure, the whole Bible is important, especially once we've digested the Gospels. But let's face it, we might get along without understanding Esther or appreciating Numbers. We might even live without the Psalms. But we couldn't get by without the apostolic witness to this central truth: Jesus of Nazareth is King of the universe.

Suggested Bible Readings

Each Gospel is a running account of the words and works of Jesus, the Christ. We tend to read it in sections, by chapters. But the chapter divisions weren't in the originals. It's a valuable experience to read a Gospel from beginning to end in one sitting.

The Gospel According to Mark

CHAPTER TWENTY

My Brother, Jesus

*B*efore I ever met my brother, I was keenly disappointed in him. Actually, it was less his fault than my parents'. By the time my brother came along I had already reached the ripe old age of "nine going on ten," and it didn't take much intelligence for me to see that he wasn't going to play catch, or swim, or stay up late talking with me. He might be a good brother, but it'd be hard for him to be much of a friend. By the time he reached the age of nine or ten, I'd probably be gone from home.

I was mulling over those regrettable facts of my brother's life while trudging off to my aunt's house. My baby brother had been born there the night before, and I'd been told I had to go see him and my mother.

I was glad to see my mother. And when my eyes swung 'round the room, I saw him. He was a very beautiful baby, his marvelous face completely framed by deep brown curls. Disappointment faded, admiration swelled, and I loved him even before I'd been allowed to hold him in my arms. In spite of my advanced years, and the fact that he'd never catch up with me, I knew then what I still know today: My brother is very special.

It's good to have relatives, brothers and sisters and aunts and uncles, but the best thing of all is to have Jesus Christ as your brother. We tend not to think of Jesus as a brother. We call Him "Lord" because He is. Savior, Christ, Messiah, and God all seem right. But calling Him "brother" seems somehow to demean

Him, as if we're trying to bring Him down to our level. What's really happening, of course, is that our brother Jesus is trying to bring us up to His level.

The Gospel of Matthew keeps reminding me that Jesus is my brother. Perhaps I should say *relative* instead of *brother*, since Jesus' relationship to me goes beyond simply being my brother. Hebrews pictures Jesus standing in front of His Father saying, "Here I am with the children that God has given me" (2:13, TEV); in that passage, He's like my father. But the idea of Jesus as our brother is predominant in the New Testament. In fact, earlier in that same chapter Jesus identifies Himself as the brother of all who believe in Him (2:11).

Two passages near the beginning of Matthew's Gospel confirm that Jesus is my brother. The first is Matthew's genealogy of Jesus, and the second is Matthew's description of Jesus' temptation.

The genealogy boldly identifies Jesus Christ as the son of Abraham and the son of David. One might think, therefore, that the genealogy of Jesus—at least in the book of Matthew—tends to divide Jesus from a large element of the human race. After all, most people are descendants of neither Abraham nor David. All the children of Abraham and David are Jews, and most people in the world, including me, are not Jewish.

But when we examine Matthew's genealogy of Jesus more closely, it becomes clear that, while Jesus was a Jew, being a descendant of Abraham is more than an ethnic characteristic. The concept "children of Abraham" is just that—it's an *idea*, a *concept*. Look at the genealogy in Matthew 1, and you can see that this is true.

Notice the careful construction with which Matthew builds the "fourteen-generations scheme" in this genealogy. This is no mere listing of the actual nation of Israel—as Nehemiah listed the names of the returning exiles in his log book. No. The genealogy of Jesus is deliberately shaped to emphasize Christ's universal role. Abraham, Jesus' father, was the universal man in whom God had promised that all the nations of the world would be blessed. David, the brilliant centerpiece of this genealogy, is the person whose kingdom was destined to become universal.

Besides, this genealogy has enough Gentile people in it to

make me see it's a mistake to think "the seed of Abraham" is defined in terms of a certain bloodline. Instead the seed of Abraham is defined in terms of covenant obedience. Rahab is in the list, and so is Bathsheba, wife of Uriah the Hittite. Ruth, the Moabitess, makes the group too. All those names give me comfort because they belong to Gentiles, and I'm a Gentile.

There's another feature of Jesus' genealogy in this Gospel that's crucial. According to Matthew, Jesus Himself isn't Abraham's descendant by blood. Matthew traces Jesus' lineage through the carpenter Joseph. It's Joseph who is the biological son of Abraham and David. Jesus wasn't biologically related to either of them because His conception was supernatural. Jesus is the only begotten Son of God, but He's one of many adopted sons of Abraham.

So this shows me that the "children of Abraham" idea is much, much larger than the group of people with Jewish blood running through their veins. I'm sure Paul was talking about this when he said later, "There is no difference between Jews and Gentiles, between slaves and free men, between men and women; you are all one in union with Christ Jesus. If you belong to Christ, then you are the descendants of Abraham and will receive what God has promised" (Gal. 3:28,29, TEV). Jesus is my brother because we are both adopted children of Abraham.

When we trace Jesus' genealogy all the way back, though, we don't stop at Abraham. We go to Adam. When I recall the awful failure our natural father made of himself, I become proud of my brother Jesus. Look at how He picked up the pieces of this ruined world and put it back together. He retraced the footsteps of the entire human race all the way back to the day my first parents were evicted from the Garden of Innocence. Jesus was not only the son of Abraham, but also the second and final Adam. He succeeded where Adam had failed so miserably. Which brings me to the second passage early in Matthew's Gospel that confirms Jesus is my brother: the temptation of Jesus.

The Old Testament began with a revelation of the cosmic battle between Satan and God, and the New Testament opens the same way. The raging fury of the demons is seen in the frustrated attempts of Herod to kill the infant Jesus. And thirty years later, just as Jesus was about to move out into the full power of His ministry, Satan came to meet Him.

The issue in Matthew 4—the chapter describing the temptation—is the same as the issue in Genesis 3: our response to the word of God. All of human history can be written in terms of this principle, "Man cannot live on bread alone, but needs every word that God speaks" (Matt. 4:4, TEV). To ignore the word that God speaks is to commit suicide; those who bind themselves to God's good word always live. Adam fell for the twisted words of Satan's promise, and we all suffered the consequences of that fall. Here, at the beginning of Jesus' ministry, the Son of Man is made to choose (again) between Satan's distorted promises and "the word that God speaks." Where Adam failed, Jesus succeeded. And there you have it—the whole gospel in a nutshell.

When I browse through the Gospel of Matthew, I'm looking into a family album. That's my "family tree" in Matthew 1. With Jesus, I've entered the great family of God's redeemed children. He has not only kept me from suicide, but has also made life worth living. My brother Jesus has even made it possible for me to go home again, to speak to my Father who is in heaven, to know that I am no orphan in this world but belong to my faithful Savior.

And the family into which Jesus brings me is consistently described by Matthew as a universal group. Brothers and sisters here are of all sorts of races, nationalities, sizes, colors, interests, cultures, backgrounds—but only one faith. The Jews who first read Matthew's Gospel must have been stunned at the multiracial character of his message.

At the very beginning of his book, Matthew painstakingly describes the visit of the Magi from the East. And it's also Matthew, the most Jewish of the Gospel writers, who carefully records Jesus' flight into Egypt. Thus, before He had turned five, Christ had accepted the worship (and even the gifts?) offered by religious leaders from Babylon, and He'd gone to the center of another great religion in Egypt. It's Matthew's intent to show that Jesus was not limited to the Hebrew race. Jesus our brother has invited into the family an indescribably mixed batch of other siblings. That's how I got in and probably how you got in as well.

It comes as no surprise that the book of Matthew concludes

with the great commission. He who has done so much for His brothers and sisters still goes with us as we lay down His gospel to examine our duty today. And I believe without doubt that there are millions in the world today who are yet to be introduced to their brother Jesus, who must be invited to join His family and ours. It is our family's business to bring them the good news as Matthew first brought it to us.

Suggested Bible Readings

The first six chapters of John's Gospel trace the initial stage of Jesus' work, from the first followers to the first deserters. Many believed when they saw the signs. Many disbelieved when they heard the words that explained the signs. The deeds were attractive; the explanation was hard to take.

The Gospel According to John 1-6

CHAPTER TWENTY-ONE

Crash Course in Christianity

Everyone has unrealized ambitions and dreams. One of mine is that I've always wanted to learn to fly but never did. That's why the ad excited my curiosity. It said: "FLAMING EVANGELIST FLIGHT SCHOOL—Learn to fly in just one week!" The school was in Missouri, and on an impulse I called it. The woman answering the telephone explained that the flight school was for evangelists and preachers only, that it would result in a student pilot's license very quickly, and that it cost "only" $400.00.

I told her it all sounded pretty good, but ventured the unsolicited opinion that the name of the school didn't exactly inspire confidence. A flaming evangelist might be a good thing on the pulpit, but the idea wasn't especially inspiring when connected so closely with flying. I'm old enough to recall the days we sang the fighting song with the dramatic line, "We rise in fame, go down in flame, nothing can stop the Army Air Corps." I decided not to sing the hymn to her over the phone, but it was this line that stirred my misgivings.

Finally, I decided to confess. I told her I might be interested if they'd consider changing the name of their school. "Oh, we couldn't do that," she replied. "We've already changed the name once. The course used to be called 'CRASH COURSE IN FLYING FOR PREACHERS.' "

With that I hung up, assured that some transcendent power meant for me to forget about flying airplanes. How could I entrust my life to instructors whose judgment in name selection was so idiotic? Flaming evangelists in the cockpit...a crash course in flying...uh uh.

There's a place for crash courses, of course, and occasionally we need them in the Christian faith. Sometimes new converts grow dramatically during a crash course; once in a while old converts do too. And Mark's Gospel is ideal for this because it includes everything we need to know about the Lord Jesus Christ —in fact, I think it contains everything we need to know to be saved. You can build your life on Mark's Gospel.

In contrast with the other Gospels, which begin with Christmas stories, Mark's short book seems to plunge into the life of Jesus almost recklessly. I've worked all the way through it several times, using it in daily 4½ minute radio broadcasts (called "Insight"), and each time I work with this material I'm impressed with how quickly Mark moves from one astonishing episode to another. There's never a pause. Reading it means rushing from one miracle to another, from one tense encounter to the next. It's not just the content of Mark's Gospel that's important; the style he uses conveys the message that *action* is the essence of Christian faith. Christians should be committed to action. Jesus was. Mark's book proves it.

If in the book of Matthew I discover that Jesus Christ is my brother, then in Mark's Gospel I see that my brother is a fighter. The person who came to occupy David's throne had a lot of David in Him. David was a fighter, you'll recall, and he came to his throne by way of struggle and bloodshed. In Mark's action-packed first chapter, Jesus' ministry is described in just three sentences: "After John had been put in prison, Jesus went to Galilee and preached the Good News from God. 'The right time has come,' he said, 'and the Kingdom of God is near! Turn away from your sins and believe the Good News!' " (1:14,15, TEV).

What stands out most in that brief summary is the idea of *kingdom*. The dominance of this theme in the New Testament is somewhat surprising because the idea as such is not directly given in the Old Testament. The Old Testament speaks of the sovereignty of God over creation and over the nation of Israel, but "the kingdom of God" is never expressly mentioned (though Daniel 7 contains related concepts). On the other hand, perhaps that's not so strange since Jesus—the Herald of that kingdom—is only seen vaguely in the Old Testament. It isn't until the New Testament that the fullness of God's saving work in Jesus is plainly revealed. And once the great Savior King appears, the kingdom of God quickly becomes visible.

The kingdom idea focuses on the worldwide struggle that has raged over our planet like a forest fire beyond control. From the beginning of the world's history, the universe has been at stake in the great fight between God and Satan. To the winner goes the prize: rule over the universe. The kingdom of Satan grew to ungainly proportions following the fall, and there were times in the tortured Old Testament history when it seemed Satan would certainly emerge the victor. At the time of Christ's birth, the whole world was in the clutches of powerful false religions, but then Jesus came, and all that changed.

The kingdom theme is not unique to Mark; it's common to all the Gospels. But the Gospel of Mark reflects the charged atmosphere of the kingdom breaking into the world in ways the other Gospels cannot match. Much of this is accomplished by Mark's style, his swift movement from one battle to another—he seems always to be describing God's blitzkrieg. Again and again in this Gospel the rule of God slashes into the claim of Satan. And when Jesus appears, the battle becomes ferocious.

Typically, when we think of battles we think of fields littered with bodies: wounded, dying, victims of the fight. But where Jesus engages in the battle, the result is healing! The miracles Jesus performed are great proofs of His kingship; the demons and their prince, Satan, hated them. In Mark you needn't go any further than chapter 1 to watch Christ begin His campaign: He exorcises an evil spirit (vss. 23-26), cools a fevered body (vss. 30,31), and cures the incurable leprosy (vss. 40-42). Such miracles demonstrate that Christ is King of all, Lord even of that territory once claimed by Satan: disease, suffering, and death.

The conflict between Jesus and the demons is of special interest these days because recent books and movies have drawn attention to demon possession. When I find Christians expressing great fear of demons, I advise them to read the Gospel of Mark.

One thing Mark makes clear is that the demon world is real.

In Jesus' encounter with the Garasene demoniac (Mark 5) we see that the demons knew Him, correctly identified Him, and felt absolutely compelled to enter a battle that would mean their own destruction. In this and other passages Mark teaches us that demons are real.

The second thing he shows us is that the nearer demons come to Jesus (or He to them), the more frantically they do their work. When the Gospel comes to pagan nations, for example, there's evidence that demons become especially active. But it's not only in pagan nations that demons work. Within the United States and Canada, for example, groups actively devoted to Satan worship do all they can to oppose Christ's children. The idea that such groups are made up of misled but harmless kooks quickly disappears when newspapers report rites requiring sexual perversions with children and altars drenched with human blood.

But the most important thing the book of Mark teaches about demons is that Jesus has absolute authority over every one of them. Because Christ is King, and His kingdom stretches over all, He is able to protect us. And because He is our brother, He wants to. The message of Mark's Gospel is clear: The kingdom of God surrounds those who surrender to the King. That message is fully as important today as it was when first the ink dried on this Gospel.

So this book crackles with the sound of conflict—sickness is overcome by the Savior and demons crumble before Him. But there's more. Another wave of opposition to Jesus was staged by the self-confident religious leaders who had captured the loyalty of the Jews.

In the seventh chapter Mark describes Jesus' expose of the Pharisees' heresy. He accuses them of replacing God's laws with manmade rules (7:7). The Pharisees, you'll recall, had developed their perversion of true religion during the years just before Jesus' birth. Much of His conflict with the religion of the Jews involved His angry opposition to the Pharisees.

In Mark's twelfth chapter we see Jesus condemn the Sadducees—masters at twisting the Old Testament message to make it say what they liked. According to the Lord, the Sadducees actually knew neither the Scriptures nor the power of God (12:24).

And I've always wondered how the scribes reacted when Jesus

told His audience, "Beware of the scribes . . . who devour widows' houses and for a pretense make long prayers" (Mark 12:38,40).

In response to all these groups, Jesus introduced the most revolutionary principle of the kingdom. He made the entrance requirements impossible for proud, haughty, condescending religious leaders: "I assure you that whoever does not receive the Kingdom of God like a child will never enter it" (10:15, TEV). With that, the pretensions of false religion were pulverized, ground into the dirt under the heel of the King—the same heel He used later to destroy the serpent's head.

The Gospel of Mark delivers a clear, precise, fast-paced description of the King and His kingdom. It makes a good crash course in the kingdom of God. And every once in a while, tired, discouraged Christians—who for one reason or another begin thinking they may as well lie down and die—should take off a couple of hours to read quickly through this tightly written book. Sometimes that's all a person needs to get up and go on serving Jesus.

Suggested Bible Readings

The middle part of John's Gospel is a story of growing conflict with "the Jews." The Pharisees were out to kill Jesus. Each confrontation increased their determination. The plan to get rid of Him took shape.

The Gospel According to John 7-12

CHAPTER TWENTY-TWO

The Special Gospel

Ask me to describe the Bible my father used when he read for our family at the table and I couldn't possibly do it. It's curious. I can still recall with tingling taste buds delicious sandwiches spread with peanut butter and Welch's grape jelly, all washed down with chocolate milk. But the picture of our family Bible has gotten away from me entirely; I don't have the slightest idea what it looked like, though it was used regularly.

Maybe it's odd, but I do recall another book. Looking back, I can see it as plainly as if it were lying on my desk right now. It was a miniature copy of the Gospel of John. I remember the cover—it was mainly blue, with a brilliant red figure of a person stamped into it. And I remember wondering why this Gospel had been printed all by itself.

Now I know.

John is special. Each of the Gospels is special, of course. But there is a quality to John's book that sets it off from the others. I don't mean it's better. No, but it's different. If we had all the other Gospels but we didn't have John's, Christianity would be substantially poorer.

That little Gospel I treasured had probably been printed by itself on the once popular theory that the Gospel of John was a good place to start into the Christian faith. If you want a person to believe and be saved, give him or her John—that was the notion. I disagree. As you know, I think Mark gives the best crash course in Christian faith. John goes best, I believe, after one has become familiar with the other Gospels. It was written considerably later than Matthew, Mark, and Luke, probably one of the last books written for the New Testament (A.D. 90?). John assumes his readers knew the information contained in the other Gospels, and he sets out to interpret that data. If our faith is shaped by the other Gospels, then as we read this special Gospel our faith is dipped in gold; it becomes shining and luminous, lustrous and rich.

I'm sure that some of the special quality of John's Gospel can be explained by his close personal attachment to Jesus Christ. He was Jesus' cousin, and his was a special relationship with the Lord. He unselfconsciously talks about himself as the disciple Jesus loved. John was close to Him at the last supper, and near enough to be picked out of the crowd by Jesus as He was being crucified. In his general letter, John stresses the intimacy he shared with Christ:

> We have heard it, and we have seen it with our eyes; yes, we have seen it, and our hands have touched it.
>
> (I John 1:1, TEV)

The "it" in this passage is the Word of life, Jesus.

We're indebted to John for personal, moving descriptions of Jesus which escaped the other Gospels. John was apparently sensitive, impressed not only with our Lord's actions, but also with His attitudes, His quiet habits, His silent glances. John noticed the blood trembling through the veins on Jesus' hands; he knew the feeling of Christ's arm slung over his shoulder as they walked together. It's John who reports Jesus' grief as He stood at the tomb of Lazarus, observing the stubborn unbelief of the people. John knew Jesus as a real human being, and that's how his Gospel portrays Him. If there are some who doubt Jesus' humanity, they must read John's book. They'll soon discover that Christ's humanity meant skin and bones, nerve endings all in place, and blood that poured out when a sword sliced through the flesh.

Because he knew Christ well, John wrote the most touching Gospel descriptions of Jesus' suffering:

> Now my heart is troubled—and what shall I say? Shall I say, "Father, do not let this hour come upon me?" But that is why I came—so that I might go through this hour of suffering.
>
> (12:27, TEV)

That Jesus came to suffer was clear. John the Baptist, seeing Jesus, immediately called Him "the Lamb of God, who takes away the sin of the world" (1:29). As the Old Testament lamb was sent into the wilderness carrying Israel's sin, the Gospel of John traces the tortured path of God's Lamb who finally carried the world's sin to the cross. And John never lets his readers forget that God's Lamb is a man, a human being. John's cousin —my brother, Jesus—had emotions that needed to be controlled, anger that needed to be held in, hurts that needed healing, and joys that needed expression. It was neither an animal nor an angel they crucified on "Good" Friday; it was a man.

This relentless emphasis on Jesus' humanity runs throughout John's Gospel. And right with it, there's the astonishing declaration that this man is, in fact, the Son of the living God. The opening sentences anchor the book squarely in God's creative work: "Before the world was created, the Word already existed; he was with God, and he was the same as God. From the very beginning the Word was with God. Through him God made all things . . ." (1:1-3, TEV).

And then the eternal Word became flesh (1:14). Stop right there. The word is *flesh*. Today's English Version, which I often use, misses the point, I think, when it says the Word became a "human being." John is talking about flesh, the flesh of sacrifice—flesh cut up, ripped and torn, boiling in a cauldron, caught on the priest's gaff hook as he goes after his supper (I Sam. 2:13,14).

What has John so fascinated is the reality of incarnation—that God somehow got into flesh. The Jesus he knew, the Jesus who was his cousin—this Jesus is God, worthy not only of a cousin's affection, but of the whole world's fervent worship. It's this apparent contradiction of terms, "God in the flesh," which John uses to represent the great mystery of union with Christ. Listen to him reporting Jesus' conversation:

> I am telling you the truth: if you do not eat the flesh of the Son of Man and drink his blood, you will not have life in yourselves. Whoever eats my flesh and drinks my blood has eternal life, and I will raise him to life on the last day.
> (John 6:53,54, TEV)

On the one hand, God had actually become flesh—He was so

fleshy that John had embraced Him. But at the same time, the "flesh and blood" Jesus was much more than muscles, glands, bones, and fluids. He was the "Lamb of God," the one whose flesh would be offered as a sacrifice for sin. To embrace Jesus, John needed only to reach out and touch Him; to be embraced by God, John needed to believe. He needed to accept the basic fact of the incarnation—first the Word had created all flesh, and then the Word had *become* flesh. That powerful message pervades the whole of John's Gospel.

And through his entire discussion of the great mystery of Christ's incarnation, John demonstrates that he is the great apostle of God's love. Though he probably wrote his Gospel as an old man, he knew firsthand what it meant both to love and to be loved by Jesus. He could look back to Jesus' baptism and recall that Jesus was loved by His Father ("This is my beloved son..."). He could remember standing at the cross, hearing Jesus direct him to Mary, knowing unmistakably then that God so loved the world He was giving His only begotten Son so that all who believed in Him could live forever.

The love God holds for the world, the love Jesus showed for His Father, the love to which Christians are called—this love is no silly sentiment, or giddy feeling. There's nothing anywhere on Calvary that looks like cheap emotionalism. What it looks like is what it is—obedience.

> I love the Father; that is why I do everything as he commands me. (14:31, TEV)

For us, as for Jesus, the key to love is obedience.

> Whoever loves me will obey my teaching. My Father will love him, and my Father and I will come to him and live with him. Whoever does not love me does not obey my teaching. (14:23,24, TEV)

And what does He ask of us?

> My commandment is this: love one another, just as I love you. The greatest love a person can have for his friends is to give his life for them. And you are my friends if you do what I command you. (15:12-14, TEV)

One of the prominent figures in John's Gospel is Thomas. Thomas, you know, was with Jesus, heard Him preach, saw His miracles, and came up doubting. Thomas was a realist, and when he saw Christ die, he decided not to believe anymore unless...well, you know the conditions he laid down.

Then Jesus came and said to Thomas,

> "Put your finger here, and see my hands; and put out your hand, and place it in my side; do not be faithless, but believing." Thomas answered him, "My Lord and my God." (20:27,28)

John tells that story right before he explains that his Gospel is for those who have *not* seen Jesus, who have not felt His arm draped over their shoulders, but who will nonetheless believe that Jesus is the Christ, the Son of God.

You understand that, don't you? It means John's Gospel was written especially for us.

Suggested Bible Readings

The last section of John's Gospel tells the intimate story of Jesus' last hours with His disciples. He tries to prepare them for the shocking events that follow. But Peter shows how unprepared they are. His declaration of undying loyalty, his denial, and his final reconciliation with the Lord are major themes of these last chapters.

The Gospel According to John 13-21

CHAPTER TWENTY-THREE

Our Heathen Friend

My friend the doctor looks at life quite differently than I do. For him surgery is exciting; for me it's terrifying. He's a specialist on the thoracic area—that's the part that stretches from under my jaw to the bottom of my rib cage. My lungs, my heart, and quite a few other parts of me are found in the thorax, and my friend is very objective about them all. I recall him once describing the thrill a surgeon experiences when leading a team through complicated open-heart surgery. As he talked, I could feel our emotions moving steadily in opposite directions: His were rising, but mine were descending rapidly. He spoke as a skilled surgeon, but I listened as a potential patient.

Part of the richness of the Christian faith is that four very different people wrote the Gospels. All were inspired by one Spirit, but each retained his unique personality. And the Gospel of Luke, as well as the book of Acts, was written by a doctor. The apostle Paul, with whom Luke spent many years, wrote from prison describing Luke as his "dear doctor" (Col. 4:14, TEV). Because of his training and practice, Luke could spot the little details that indicate a person's health or illness. His was a curious mind, with a certain bent for detail and a devotion to solid evidence; these qualities are obvious in his precise records.

But Luke's value for us is not first of all in his concern for precision. All of the Bible is precisely as it ought to be—God has seen to that. What Luke provides that is unique among the Gospel writers is his background: He almost certainly came directly from heathenism into the Christian faith. He was neither born a Jew nor converted to the Jewish religion. He was, frankly, a heathen. When I describe him as a heathen, I don't mean to suggest he was a primitive who worshiped rocks; he was, rather, a man who had drunk deeply from the fountain of the finest heathen culture. His Greek was superb—literary and artistic. Luke was a noble representative of the best of the pagan world. He would have made a wonderful heathen friend. But somewhere along the expanding edge of the world-conquering Christian faith, the power of the gospel touched his life and changed him.

Do you sometimes wonder how we can attract unbelievers to Jesus Christ? Just read Luke. He'll tell you. He came by that route. Where did it happen? Some say Antioch. I think more likely it was Philippi. I think Luke was in the crowd as Paul preached, and God captured a physician for His service. There's no record of the shock waves sent through his life, the friends or family he left to follow Jesus. But it's clear he left whatever practice he had established to accompany the missionary Paul. Luke was on the ship with Paul when he sailed for Rome; he wrote the stirring firsthand account of the storm and shipwreck.

Of all the Gospel accounts of Jesus' life, death, and resurrection, Luke's is the most detailed and complete. And his description of the early expansion of the church ("The Acts of the Apostles") still shapes the church today. If we were to rename Luke's books, we might call them *The Acts of Jesus* and *The Acts of Jesus' Church*. Jesus' work capped off the entire Old Testament activity of God, and Luke's Gospel chronicles the words and deeds of the Messiah. The New Testament church capped off the work of Jesus, and Luke's Acts of the Apostles reports the extension of Christ's ministry through His church. As Christ must not be divided from the Old Testament, the church must not be divided from Christ—and Luke's double-barreled writing underscores that point.

Among the first five books of the New Testament, it's the two messages of Luke that most dramatically demonstrate the great power of the preaching of the Word of God. Those who've studied the book of Acts carefully have detailed the various "mission speeches" found there. From the astonishing sermon of

Peter on Pentecost to Paul's Mars Hill speech designed so carefully to sway a heathen audience, the messages are all similar. The preachers were never ashamed to repeat the basic gospel claims. Whatever people were in the audience, Jews or Gentiles, they needed to hear Jesus preached. The facts of His life, death, resurrection, and ascension were announced again and again. And in response, God brought people into His church.

It still works that way. As I write this, there's a letter on my desk from mainland China, a response to the same message that converted Luke and is now preached over the radio. Would you like to read what our listener wrote?

> I am a young worker. A few days ago I happened to tune to your religious program "Good News for the Whole World" [the Chinese broadcast of the Back to God Hour]. My heart was suddenly cleared up and I realized that there is such a great and beautiful religion in the world—Christianity.
>
> In the past several days, I have been listening regularly to your program. The more I listened to it, the greater my interest became, as though enchanted. In my twenty odd years of life, except for a few snatches about Christianity as described in some novels, I may say that I have been totally ignorant about Christ. Before God I am truly a blind man, not able to know the Lord, to believe in or love the Lord.
>
> Now I very much hope to know about Christian doctrines, about forms of worship, and about everything a sincere believer should know....

I believe people, like this Chinese man, are converted today because what Luke wrote in his Gospel is the truth, and because the church is still preaching the message outlined in the Acts of the Apostles. In the writings of Luke, the convert, we hear the call to conversion which still rings 'round the world today.

Because he wrote not only a Gospel, but also the Acts, it's particuarly in Luke's writings that we see the miracles of Jesus continued in Jesus' church. The great miracles of faith which Jesus once performed were now performed by His apostles. As thousands of people were swept into the newborn church, they witnessed stunning miracles of healing, even of raising the dead.

The crowds who had once followed Jesus now trailed the apostles. And when the apostles spoke, the crowds who hounded them heard a message which was centered on the resurrection of Jesus and inspired by the Spirit of Christ.

How important were the miracles to the ministry of the apostles? I believe they were crucial, establishing the fact that the apostles' work was, indeed, a continuation of the work of Jesus. Nothing could have more certainly convinced the crowds that "this Jesus whom you crucified" was raised, ascended, and made Lord over all. Some people insist that miracles can be performed by the church today just as they were by the apostles then. I don't think so—though I heartily believe God can do all things. I believe the apostles' miracles were necessary proof for the claims of the gospel at that particular point in history. The miracles not only restored health, returned life, or gained the apostles' release from jail—they also confirmed that the power of Christ had not been diminished by the cross and that the Spirit of God had, in fact, been poured out on the church.

The miracles which have special significance for us today are not, it seems to me, those disputed claims of possible healing that occur under questionable circumstances. In most cases such debatable reports do as much to challenge our faith as to confirm it. The miracles confidently reported by the physician Luke, on the other hand, have enormous value for us because these miracles belong to the church *as church*. I think of the forty-year-old man who'd never walked, leaping and dancing around Peter and John as they tried to explain the power of Jesus to the Jewish rulers—and I laugh. This miracle belongs to me and to my church. There's no question that it happened, no debated reports which merely fuel the arguments of skeptics. It's a simple miracle, performed by the church, done in the power of God's Spirit—the same power by which we preach, and pray, and receive new members (even from mainland China) today.

And we see it all today because there was another miracle first: There was this heathen physician, you see, whose name was Luke . . . .

Acts may be a one-spirit show (Jesus' Spirit), but it's never a one-man show. Even when the later chapters focus on one apostle (Paul), he's never alone. The believers worked as a team, "while the Lord worked with them."

Acts 13-19:20; Mark 16:9-20

CHAPTER TWENTY-FOUR

Don't Throw This Letter Away

An influential British author often concluded letters he'd written to his friends, his wife, and his lovers with the request, "Please destroy this letter." Those who knew him best suspected that, in fact, the writer fervently hoped not a sentence would be lost. Apparently the author, D. H. Lawrence, was convinced of his own talent and believed that someday every letter he'd penned would be very valuable. Because most of those to whom he wrote understood what Lawrence meant, the letters of this sensitive, brilliant, and thoroughly pagan author have been collected and published. Together they provide a powerful portrait of a colorful man.

Some letters, though, *are* best destroyed. I know a soldier who, after returning from overseas to marry the girl he loved, ceremoniously burned the letters he'd written while they were apart for two years. Both bride and groom were relieved that their letter-writing days were past, and they were delighted to officially, symbolically, put those days behind them.

Have you ever considered how much of Christian doctrine is built on a collection of writings that are essentially letters? Twenty-one of the New Testament books fall into this category, and they make up about a third of its length. That so much of our faith is rooted in letters says something extremely interesting about both the Bible and our religion.

Whatever else letters may be, they are nearly always the most personal form of writing:

Dear Marie,

Would you believe it—Rick *finally* asked me for a date!!!!

Dear Son,

This will be a very difficult letter to write. The doctor met with your mother and me a few minutes ago....

Dear Greg,

The water's warm, the beach is great, and you're out of your skull if you don't come for the weekend!

That's the way letters begin, and they usually become even more personal as they go along. Most of us have even used letters at some point in our lives to communicate something too personal or too difficult to talk about in person. We pour out words on paper that we could not pour out in any other way.

Now think of it: This intimate, personal, often emotional form of writing covers one out of every three pages in the New Testament.

This makes the Bible radically different from sacred books of other religions. The Mohammedan *Koran*, for example, is said to have been dictated to Mohammed by Allah. There's none of Mohammed in it at all. It sounds like it fell from the sky: It's other-worldly, remote, and exaggerated. In contrast, much of our sacred book began as letters written to another man or woman or church. And letters, even here, are powerfully human.

But is there really much resemblance between, say, the book of Romans and the kind of letters we write today? Maybe not. But they're both letters. We generally call the letters in the Bible "epistles," and that makes some difference. Epistles are letters written for public circulation. A letter appearing in the newspaper, "An Open Letter to the Mayor," is an epistle because it's written to be published openly; many more people than just the mayor will read it. In the same way "letters to the editor," meant for publication, are really "epistles to the public."

The twenty-one letters we have in the New Testament are all epistles, meant to be read by a larger audience than the person or group listed in the heading. What's more, they were written not only for people living in the authors' days, but also for us.

The epistles from Paul, John, Peter, and James were meant for the eyes of Christ's followers today, as surely as Luke's books were not intended to be the private possessions of Theophilus. By calling them "epistles," we're saying these letters were written for public consumption.

But if we want to interpret these books carefully, faithfully, listening closely to what God is saying, we also must remember that all epistles are, first of all, letters. Like all letters, epistles are written under specific circumstances, for certain reasons, by a particular person, to a definite audience. They are deeply historical—that is, related to the time and place in which they are written. If we forget these facts, we demean the Bible by treating it as if it were the *Koran*. The miracle of the Bible's inspiration is that the Spirit worked *through* human beings, not apart from them. And that's wonderfully apparent when we read the New Testament epistles.

There's a great contrast, for example, between Paul's epistle to the Romans and his letter to Philemon. I have a feeling Paul thought for a very long time about what he would write to the church in Rome. A friend of mine, a long-distance runner, once told me how much thinking he did during his daily run. Paul had his "daily run" too. He spent some days at sea, looking over the waves, thinking and praying, and other days logging overland miles by foot or horseback or donkey. I think it was while he traveled that Paul thought of the errors in Rome that needed to be corrected, the people there who deserved to be praised, and the things he should say in a letter before he came in person. I once described Romans as a letter that took Paul many "miles" to write, and I think that's right.

But the letter to Philemon—like Ephesians, Philippians, Colossians—was written in a jail cell. Paul expresses some of his own personal needs as a prisoner. And in his last letter to "his son" Timothy, Paul writes as an old man, imprisoned, ill, and fearful that he'll not survive the cold and damp of winter. He begs Timothy to come soon, to stop by Troas on the way and pick up Paul's coat, books, and parchments which he'd left there with Carpus. And then, Paul adds once more, "Do your best to come before winter" (II Tim. 4:21, TEV).

The fact that these epistles are so full of personal references

115

gives them great character. But sometimes these references are so deeply buried in the time and place of the letters that the points become unclear to us today. Think, for instance, of Paul's reference to baptizing people for the dead (I Cor. 15:29). The Mormons have built a great deal of their religion on that obscure passage. I don't have any idea what it actually means (nor, I think, do the Mormons). But I'm sure Paul knew what he had in mind, and the Corinthian Christians understood his message.

All of the New Testament letters stress the divine origin of their message. Peter, James, and John knew Jesus intimately. And Paul, when writing to the Galatians, assures his readers that his message "is not of human origin" (Gal. 1:11, TEV). Each of the authors was specially qualified to speak for the Lord. As the Gospels are God-given records of Jesus' life, death, and resurrection, so these letters, steeped in the history of the infant church, explain the significance of these great acts of God for all of us. They are not treatises on dogmatics, nor formal expressions of Christian theology. Neither are they in catechism form. They are, instead, intensely personal, historical, God-given, and true.

For all the grand significance of the epistles' contents, and for all the stress we place on their authors' special qualifications, these letters are also important because they teach us the special humanness which is so unique to both the Christian religion and the book on which it's founded. They remind us that our faith has not been established through the work of supermen and superwomen, but through the lives of real people who knew the despair of a broken heart and the ache of longing for the kiss of a dear one.

The letters we have are a stirring collection of Christian teaching, straight from the hearts of special writers who put words to parchment in prison cells, in rented quarters, and while traveling down a Macedonian highway. By studying the letters, we come to know the writers well. And the better we know them, the more inclined we become to make their testimony our own.

I once bent low over an aged woman's bed. She was dying. She was eager to be with Christ. I could hardly make out what she was saying. And then I recognized it: "I know whom I have believed, and am persuaded that He is able to keep that which I've committed...." Her testimony was the same as Paul's. All her life she'd been reading the letters he'd written to her; she'd never thrown them away.

Those letters have also come to me. And to you.

Suggested Bible Readings
Freedom was a precious privilege in an age of slavery. People didn't like being told they were slaves (of sin or of the law). But Paul follows Jesus in teaching that true freedom comes only by faith in God's Son.

Galatians; John 8:31-59

CHAPTER TWENTY-FIVE

God's Kind of Religion

I've learned in my work at the Back to God Hour that I shouldn't look at the day's mail if I have a lot to do. When there are heavy production demands (television at 10:30, radio recording at 11:30, writing to be finished by the end of the day), reading letters people send in can ruin me. I wait until the work is done, or until the next day when the schedule is less rushed.

I adopted this peculiar habit several years ago when I finally admitted, more to myself than anyone else, that letters really affect me. I can't ignore a comment or dismiss a criticism. Each writer is very convinced that he or she has something special to say to me, and so am I. If the letters are complimentary, as they sometimes are, it boosts my morale to read them. But in each batch of letters there's apt to be at least one that takes sharp issue with something I've written or said. Those letters always hit me hard. If I think the criticism is wrong, I can't postpone framing my reply, explaining my defense. But sometimes I have to agree that the writer is right, and I start berating myself: "How could you be so stupid, Nederhood?" The point is, my mail significantly influences my work, and since I can't afford to lose a whole day's production to one letter, I'm careful about when I read my correspondence.

The letters in the New Testament can be mighty disturbing too. They show us God's kind of religion, and God's kind of religion can change our lives. Unlike humanity's kind of religion, which is often designed as an escape, something to turn us away from the world in which we live, God's kind of religion is deeply interested in human problems. When I read the letters in the Bible, it becomes abundantly clear that to be "religious" as a Christian means to be actively involved with other people. Let me show you what I mean by looking at the letters from John, James, and Peter.

The first epistle of John tells us that, when all is said and done, God makes lovers out of those who love Jesus Christ. A grim perversion has so contaminated our world that we can scarcely speak of love without a twinge of embarrassment. But if there's one word that captures everything true about the Christian faith, it's *love*. God's love explains why He created the world and why He's interested in saving it. And He expects that we, His images, will love as He loves.

So central to faith is love that John makes it the basic test: "We know that we have left death and come over into life; we know it because we love our brothers" (I John 3:14, TEV). What makes the claim so startling is its simplicity. If someone says he or she believes in Jesus, but hates people, that person lies. Those who love Jesus love His brothers and sisters. No exceptions? No exceptions. And if you think I'm overstating the case, then listen to John:

> Dear friends, if this is how God loved us, then we should love one another.... God is love, and whoever lives in love lives in union with God and God lives in union with him....We love because God first loved us. If someone says he loves God, but hates his brother, he is a liar ....The command that Christ has given us is this: whoever loves God must love his brother also.
>
> (I John 4:11,16,19,20,21, TEV)

John announces that if we are truly Christian, we will love. And then along comes James who stuns us by saying flat out that a faith without works is dead. Dead faith, like a dead horse, won't get you anywhere at all.

James is careful to avoid the heresy which Pharisees had made their theme; no one can make himself or herself into a righteous person. We're good at refuting that error, too, so we're comfortable when James reminds his readers: " 'Abraham believed God, and because of his faith God accepted him as righteous.' And so

Abraham was called God's friend" (James 2:23, TEV). So far, nothing James has said will shake us up.

But wait a minute. Look at that quotation in its whole context. Here's what James actually said:

> How was our ancestor Abraham put right with God? It was through his actions, when he offered his son Isaac on the altar. Can't you see? His faith and his actions worked together; his faith was made perfect through his actions. And the scripture came true that said, "Abraham believed God, and because of his faith God accepted him as righteous." And so Abraham was called God's friend. You see, then, that it is by his actions that a person is put right with God, and not by his faith alone.   (James 2:21-24, TEV)

That's a troubling passage for many people. They think they need to argue with James, to teach him that we are justified by faith, not works. But the letter of James is no less inspired than any text from Paul. What James says about the demand for works is absolutely right and not particularly different from what John says about love. Unless we are busy doing what God does (loving, working), we may not claim to have faith. The Christian religion does not lift us away from the world, making us mystics who see some abstract truths. On the contrary: "Religion that is pure and undefiled before God and the Father is this: to visit orphans and widows in their affliction, and to keep oneself unstained from the world" (James 1:27).

Neither James nor John leaves any doubt that if we say we believe in God, we are inviting others to examine our compassion, our love, and our works of mercy. If there's no evidence of our faith, we should do some powerful self-examination.

But it isn't simply a matter of what I must do, how much my love should reflect Christ's. While there is much that Christianity does for and to the individual person, this religion does not exalt the individual. In fact, to become Christian means we will lose whatever sense of individual identity we once had and must accept a shockingly new corporate identity. Can you imagine going to sleep Dutch and waking up Chinese? How about being Black for thirty years, and then showing up White one day? That would radically challenge any sense of self-identity. And that's exactly how Peter describes the new identity we find in

120

Christ—as a new race: "But you are the chosen race, the King's priests, the holy nation, God's own people, chosen to proclaim the wonderful acts of God, who called you out of darkness into his own marvelous light" (I Pet. 2:9, TEV).

There's a great deal we could say about this new (chosen) race, this new (holy) nation. You know it's not a race built along bloodlines; the new "seed of Abraham" comes from the many races of the world. And this new "nation" is really a "nation within all nations," a band of Jesus' followers who owe their ultimate allegiance to the King of Calvary. This nation is defined by grace, not geography.

In his letter to Philippi, a fiercely patriotic Roman colony where retired army captains often spent their days, the apostle Paul reminded his readers that they were citizens of heaven (3:20). We are too. And when we read the letters from John, James, and Peter, and put together their messages—that we must love, work, and be a holy nation—then we begin to sense our calling in this world. We go beyond the question, "What must I do to be saved?" Now we ask, "What must *we* do *because* we're saved?"

One thing we must do is speak out for justice in the countries where our "holy nation" is housed. There's one evil so heinous and perverse we can hardly believe it's being practiced widely, but it is: abortion. We must act to end such horrifying deeds. We must develop life-styles that free us from bondage to material things. How can we be free to seek justice if we are slaves to money and the things it can buy? We are called not simply to be individuals who try not to cuss, or who keep our hands at home when we date. We are called to be a people with a shining sense of justice and righteousness, who together speak out critically against evil, who collectively work hard for just change.

In Canada and the States some Christians are currently working together to make Christian schools available to all children. Their argument is simple: We are God's nation and God's nation, of course, has its own schools. These schools are, in fact, an expression of social dissent, one form of collective Christian opposition to the country's values. In working to establish such institutions, we insist that the kingdom must come right now, in our time, before the startled eyes of all who have not yet submitted to Christ.

Citizens in God's special nation have often been put in difficult positions. It can be dangerous to point out massive hypocrisies in the highest reaches of government. People are sometimes jailed for opposing foolish or unjust policies of national defense. But with God's Spirit, surely we can find courage enough to protest the continued slaughter of the unborn, the foreign policies which create hunger rather than justice, and the programs of national "defense" which encourage dishonorable aggression.

We begin by having the courage to submit to Christ, making Him our King. Entirely. Then we must take up our cross and follow. That's God's kind of religion, and it will someday change the world!

Suggested Bible Readings

James writes a very practical letter; but practical doesn't mean common sense. His advice is very uncommon. Anyone who decides to walk the new, Christian way must do it completely and single-heartedly. It's all or nothing. Count the cost and then do what you say, act out what you believe.

The letter of James; Luke 14:25-35

CHAPTER TWENTY-SIX

Theopneustos

Sorry about that. But *theopneustos* it is. You say it this way: *theo* (rhymes with "Leo"), *p* (just a little "pa"), *neus* (same as the hangman's "noose"), *tos* (like a throw, a "toss"). Put it together and you have theo-pa-noose-toss, only it's spelled *theopneustos*. And *theopneustos* is the key word if we're to understand how we must read the Bible.

Some words can't be translated from one language to another. The French talk about "television"—but they hate themselves for it, because the last thing they want is an English word in the vocabulary of France. The Dutch speak about "baby-sitting." Baby-sitting is baby-sitting—it's untranslatable. So is *theopneustos*. Paul used *theopneustos* when he wrote Timothy and told him about the Bible:

> All Scripture is *theopneustos* and is useful for teaching the truth, rebuking error, correcting faults, and giving instruction for right living, so that the person who serves God may be fully qualified and equipped to do every kind of good deed. (II Tim. 3:16,17, TEV)

Does *theopneustos* actually appear in your Bible? No. That untranslatable word does have an English equivalent, although not an exact or entirely accurate one. The English "translation" of *theopneustos* is "inspired by God." Normally,when we speak of an "inspired book," the focus is on the *book*. But in the Bible, the idea of *theopneustos* carries emphasis away from the book and fastens it on God. *Theopneustos* begins with the word *God*—

theo(s). The rest of the word really means "breathed." To say that the Bible is *theopneustos* is really to say that the Bible has been *ex*pired rather than *in*spired; it is exhaled by God. The Bible is *theopneustos*, the God-breathed book.

The reason I'm fussing over this strange word is my conviction that all true religion is rooted in this special book. Human thought has shaped a great deal of religion over the years. Scientific geniuses have made the religious news frequently. And our own feelings, our emotional responses to words and people and events, have often moved to center stage in the drama of human religion.

But the fact is, neither human thought, nor scientific discovery, nor unbridled human emotion will get you the true religion. I have thousands of years of hard evidence to prove I'm right. There is only one true religion, and it's God's; there is only one place to discover that religion, and it's in God's exhaled, *theopneustos* book. If that seems at all difficult or complicated, I can say it much more simply:

> Jesus loves me, this I know,
> For *the Bible* tells me so.

I trust the Bible. I'm willing to stake my life on it.

Some people believe it's foolishly outdated to call the Bible the Word of God. I don't think it's strange at all. In fact, I think it's by far the most reasonable explanation for the Bible's peculiar qualities. The fact that this book is God-breathed explains why many authors, working over a 1,300-year period of time, could so consistently describe and interpret the mighty acts of God. Anyone who knows the Bible at all knows that when you hold the Bible in your hand, you're holding a miracle. Writing this book has reminded me again of what a miracle the Bible is, and *theopneustos* explains how it happened.

The idea of *theopneustos* is not nearly so vague as it may first seem. When we speak of the breath of God in connection with writing the Bible, we're speaking of the Holy Spirit's work. "For no prophetic message ever came just from the will of man, but men were under the control of the Holy Spirit as they spoke the message that came from God" (II Pet. 1:21, TEV).

We're living in a time of enormous confusion regarding the work of the Holy Spirit. It has become popular for unstable people to mistakenly assume that their emotional binges are Spirit-induced. Claiming some special ministry of the Holy Spirit, both men and women have led others into deadly spiritual perversions. "Having the Holy Ghost" becomes a way of putting oneself beyond all laws and judgments (who can criticize the Spirit?). Being "possessed of the Spirit" becomes an excuse for erratic, sometimes even criminal, behavior ("God told me to do it," confessed the mass murderer).

But that's not right, of course. To be genuinely possessed by God's Spirit is to acknowledge that we possess, and are possessed by, His *book*. The Bible is the great work of God's Holy Spirit who moved through the lives of prophets and apostles, who carefully preserved and presented us with the message that comes from God Himself. The Spirit doesn't work in contradiction to what He wrote. If you want to know what the Spirit wants of you, read the Bible. If you want to experience the benefits of the Spirit's ministry, bind yourself to His book.

I'm convinced that the Christian life must be based entirely on the Bible, that true Christians are characterized by an undying fascination with the Bible. When I say that, I open myself to the criticism of Bible worship or "bibliolatry." That danger's real, and I know about it. But there are only a few chapters left, and I want to be blunt with you. I believe one must make a choice, a faith choice, either for or against the Bible. Either God produced this book through His Holy Spirit, or He did not. If He didn't, close this book as well as that one, and go looking for hope somewhere else. If He did, believe and obey. There isn't, I think, any middle ground between accepting or dismissing the Bible's claims about itself. You simply have to decide about *theopneustos*, true or false, right or wrong. If you've made *that* decision, and you are convinced that this book comes from God, *then* you must go on to avoid the danger of bibliolatry.

There are certainly effective guards against Bible worship. The most obvious defense is the Holy Spirit Himself, the Bible's primary author. The great work of the Spirit is to point believers to Jesus Christ. So the Spirit-produced book keeps Christ in the very center. As Christ Himself said, "The Helper, the Holy Spirit, whom the Father will send in my name, will teach you everything and make you remember all that I have told you"

(John 14:26, TEV). The Holy Spirit points us away from Himself to the Father and the Son. Similarly, His book—the Bible—points us away from itself to God.

I should add, however, that those who actually worship the Bible are outnumbered at least a hundred to one by those who ignore it completely. Using a Bible as mere table decoration, or as a book to stand on the shelf, is more common in most modern homes than putting it on a pedestal and bowing before it in worship. It's rare that the Word of God suffers from too much esteem.

But always, down through the ages, the Bible has been regarded with reverence by at least some members of each generation. In the Old Testament era and the time of the early church, dedicated scribes carefully preserved each letter and word. During the Middle Ages, monks labored in damp and drafty cells, spending tedious years transcribing this book with loving care. New discoveries, such as the "Dead Sea Scrolls," have confirmed that the text has been remarkably well preserved over thousands of years.

In addition to preservation—which is also a work of the Spirit—there has long been a great deal of interest in translating the Bible from the original into the languages of the people. This can be an exasperating task, but God has continually raised up men and women who have been willing to exhaust themselves so that common people could read God's Word.

What all this shows, finally, is that to call the Bible *theopneustos* is to say more than simply how it came into being. The God-breathed book is not only unique in how it came to be written, but also in how it comes to us. It has been graciously retained by the Spirit who wrote it, and in His power it comes to us today. As certainly as the Galilean crowds needed to decide about the carpenter's Son from Nazareth—"Is He the One?"—we must decide about the Spirit's book, the Bible. We are not called to worship it, only to believe it and obey.

May God give us the grace to do exactly that.

Suggested Bible Readings

Paul urges young Timothy to train in godliness. His training food must be "the words of faith and of the good doctrine." The man of God lives by the Word of God. He recognizes in it the voice of the Good Shepherd and follows that voice.

The First Letter of Paul to Timothy; John 10:22-42

CHAPTER TWENTY-SEVEN

The Point of No Return

When I think of the late actor John Wayne, I don't think about cowboys, gunfighters, or Vietnam Green Berets. I think about "The High and the Mighty." It's an old film about an old plane, a "prop" DC-6, and a veteran airline pilot who lost his nerve during a long night flight from Honolulu to Los Angeles. Before the film ended, I walked out. I couldn't stand the suspense. I was flying in those old airplanes regularly, and I didn't enjoy the terror on the screen. It wasn't until years later, watching a tired rerun on TV, that I found out Wayne and his passengers had actually made it. After more than a decade, I was finally relieved. Do you know what stood out in my memory all those years—and still does? The sweat pouring down John Wayne's forehead as his airplane approached "the point of no return."

"The point of no return" is an interesting spot for those who cross the ocean. Up to that point it's possible to turn back in case anything goes wrong. After that point the only choice is to keep going; turning back would be certain disaster.

There's a point like that in the Christian faith. The book of Hebrews describes it and warns those who are inclined to head back that they've passed the point of no return:

> You have not come, as the people of Israel came, to what you can feel, to Mount Sinai with its blazing fire, the darkness and the gloom, the storm, the blast of a trumpet, and the sound of a voice....Instead, you have come to

Mount Zion and to the city of the living God, the heavenly Jerusalem, with its thousands of angels. You have come
to the joyful gathering of God's first-born sons, whose
names are written in heaven.   (Heb. 12:18,19,22,23, TEV)

The book of Hebrews was written to Jewish Christians who
felt the irresistible tug of their old religion and were tempted to
go back to ancient traditions. They'd come past the Calvary hill
and the empty tomb, the point of no return, but still they were
thinking of turning back.

There's an air of mystery about this book, enhanced by the
fact that we don't know its author. There are times it seems the
writer must have been Paul; it's easy to see why the Belgic Confession names him. I feel comfortable thinking it could have
been Apollos who had been instructed by Paul. Certainly it was
someone steeped in the apostolic gospel circulated in the early
church.

But the author was also well versed in the Old Testament literature and faith. He was thoroughly familiar with the covenants, new and old, with the early promises of God and the new
promises established through the Lord Jesus Christ. Journal-
ists like Hal Lindsey, and books like his *Late Great Planet Earth*,
have stimulated a renewed and feverish interest in things Jewish
in our day. And if *we're* interested in Old Testament prophecy
now, it's easy to imagine why Jewish Christians of the first century were attracted to the religion in which they'd been born.
The author of Hebrews understood it all.

Some of Paul's writings, Galatians for example, argue
strenuously against the Pharisees' heresy of salvation through
the works of law. Paul, who'd been a Pharisee himself, was
unalterably opposed to it. But it's not this heresy we find wooing
the Christians to whom Hebrews was written.

They were fascinated by Old Testament religion at its best, the
faith reestablished by Nehemiah among returning exiles, the vision that rebuilt the temple and reinstated the temple service.
Solid Jewish theology caught the imagination of these Jewish
Christians, and they started looking back fondly at Old Testament ritual and liturgy.

Hebrews warns against looking back; since Christ's work is
finished, the Christian church has passed the point of no return.

129

All that was instituted in the Old Testament era, including the activities related to temple worship, was temporary. After Jesus, it's gone, and there's no going back again. The superiority of Christ and His sacrifice dominates the book of Hebrews. After seeing His brilliance, Old Testament worship looks dull and gray. Hebrews expresses it well:

> My Christian brothers, who also have been called by God! Think of Jesus, whom God sent to be the High Priest of the faith we profess. He was faithful to God, who chose him to do this work, just as Moses was faithful in his work in God's house . . . . Moses was faithful in God's house as a servant, and he spoke of the things that God would say in the future. But Christ is faithful as the Son in charge of God's house. We are his house if we keep up our courage and our confidence in what we hope for. (3:1,2,5,6, TEV)

With these words the author tries to turn the attention of the Hebrew Christians away from the past toward the great hope ahead. Their hope faded when Christ did not return as soon as they expected. It was probably comforting for them to go back and reenact those events that the Old Testament people had carried out while waiting for the Messiah. It gave them a sense of history, of belonging to God's chosen people. But these rituals, so impressive in the days before Christ, had become foolish and even dangerous in the age of the new covenant.

In Hebrews we find one of the Bible's strongest antidotes to the human tendency to idolize the past, ignoring both the present and the future. It delivers this corrective in three ways.

First, it explains the place of rituals which seemed so terribly important in the Old Testament era. Take the furnishings of the tabernacle, for instance.

> Those things, which are copies of the heavenly originals, had to be purified in that way But the heavenly things themselves require much better sacrifices. For Christ did not go into a man-made Holy Place, which was a copy of the real one. He went into heaven itself, where he now appears on our behalf in the presence of God. (Heb. 9:23,24)

I've sometimes wondered why God paid such careful attention to various details of the tabernacle. Why would the God who created all things care about the color of the hangings in the tabernacle, or the way the priests dressed? And how exactly were the sacrifices related to forgiveness? I still can't answer every question, but Hebrews assures me that the answers lie not in the Old Testament descriptions, but in the heavenly realities. They were images, "copies of the heavenly originals." I begin to understand when I see, for example, that the Old Testament sacrificial lamb was an image, a pre-reflection, of Jesus—the Lamb of God on the cross.

The second thing Hebrews stresses is that the past *is* past. The old way of doing things is over. The sacrifice to end all sacrifices has been made. This may be the strongest material in the Bible against the Roman Catholic mass. The mass is designed to be a continuation of Jesus' sacrifice, a redoing in the present of what Christ has done in the past. It's an attempt to extend, to prolong the suffering that has ended. The Roman Catholic mass, therefore, is judged harshly by the book of Hebrews.

I certainly don't say this because I dislike Roman Catholics. On the contrary, I'm deeply impressed by many Catholics and much of their faith. But I also believe we should know why we're Protestant, if we are; either that, or we should prepare to rejoin the great Roman Catholic Church. It is, after all, deeply appealing and entirely right on many counts. But in the book of Hebrews I find a compelling reason to remain Protestant: The past is past. We have gone beyond the point of no return. To reenact the scene from Calvary is as futile, and fatal, as going back to the faith of Nehemiah.

The third thing the book of Hebrews shows is how the two covenants, old and new, are related. It does that from the very beginning:

> In many and various ways God spoke of old to our fathers by the prophets; but in these last days he has spoken to us by a Son.... (Heb. 1:1,2)

The great message of this book is that God, who spoke to us through Abraham our father, Moses our law-giver, David our chorister, and Isaiah our prophet, has now spoken to us in "son." That's literally what it says in the original language. It's not "a son." It's not even "the son." It's simply "son." Sometimes we speak in words. Sometimes we speak in gestures. Sometimes God speaks one way and sometimes another; but ultimate-

131

ly He speaks *in son*. The covenant promised in the Garden of Eden is finally brought to the Garden of Gethsemane. The word of promise to Abraham was fulfilled stunningly the moment Mary caught her breath and mumbled first to herself, "I think...He's risen."

But even *that* is not the grand finale. Hebrews takes the covenant all the way to heaven, and brings us along to have a look. And do you know what we see there? We see Jesus in the company of all His brothers and sisters, all His "children." No longer humbled or broken or bleeding, He stands proudly before His Father in heaven, and with His arms outstretched He calls out loudly, "Here I am with all the children that you've given me" (cf. Heb. 2:9-13). Jesus is like the maestro who, at the close of the concert, gestures grandly, presenting his orchestra to the applauding audience.

One day all the world will see Jesus standing before His Father. Then all will know that the author of Hebrews was exactly right: Anyone who has been with Christ has long ago passed the point of no return. What's more, who'd want to go back?

Suggested Bible Readings

The Bible pictures a continuity of God's dwelling with His people. But the old city, Jerusalem, with its gardens has been replaced by the heavenly Jerusalem, the garden city of the living God. We may never go back. We must move with the Bible from garden to garden, from old city to new.

Genesis 2:8-9,15-17; 3:21-23; Matthew 26:36-48; John 19:41; 20: 11-16; Revelation 22:1-5

CHAPTER TWENTY-EIGHT

From Silence to Sound

*F*or centuries the Bible has enthralled those who've faithfully read it. The Old Testament, the Old Covenant, the Old Promise; the New Testament, the New Covenant, the New Promise—the Bible is the *theopneustos* book, the Word God breathed for us. And it has, so nearly as I can tell, only one defect. The Bible is silent. It's as silent as a stone.

Before I close this book, I want you to know there will be a day when that silence will be shattered by the sound of the trumpets and the sound of the voices.

> Then the seventh angel blew his trumpet, and there were loud voices in heaven, saying, "The power to rule over the world belongs now to our Lord and his Messiah, and he will rule forever and ever!" (Rev. 11:15, TEV)

I've only recently accepted the fact that I find the book of Revelation exceptionally hard to understand. At first it was a disappointment. I remember one rainy Pennsylvania morning when a group of young people implored me to explain John's Revelation to them. They were so eager I had to agree, but later when we sat in a lonely, damp cabin and I talked to them, their faces fell. They realized I was nearly as ignorant as they were. "It's apocalyptic," I said dismally. "I mean, it's different—it's different from most of the Bible; it's peculiarly Jewish writing, and it's very hard to understand precisely. I know what Hal Lindsey says. I know.... But he's wrong. We can't make perfect identifications between things in this book and things in our modern world. We can't. But I can't help you much." And they were obviously very disappointed. So was I.

But lately I've begun to think that Revelation is a book to be savored and tasted and felt. Why do we think we have to understand everything in the Bible? Some of it we must let wash over our lives, giving us vitality from its sheer force. Revelation is like that. Revelation tells me the day will come when we will be able to exchange the Bible's sometimes exasperating silence for the clear, jewellike tone of the trumpet. We will hear the voices of the twenty-four elders announcing that Jesus is Lord over all. We will watch knees bend all around and hear every tongue confess that Jesus is Lord.

When I read the book of Revelation, I get the sense that heaven is really not very far away. I have the impression that heavenly reality is very close, that being in touch with it is more a matter of opening one's eyes, or having one's eyes opened, than anything else. The glorious Jesus who appears in the first chapter of Revelation gives no impression of having completed an immense journey. Seeing Him is simply a matter of turning around and looking (1:12,13). And before, when John had seen Jesus ascend into heaven, he hadn't watched Jesus soar forever up into space. No, a cloud had received Him out of John's sight—and clouds often symbolized the presence of God, not His absence. At the most, heaven's just the other side of the "cloud."

I think it would be wrong to picture heaven as infinitely far away, making the scenes in the book of Revelation seem as if they're on another planet. We must continuously remind ourselves that heaven is real—as real as the Bible, or this book, or the eyes with which you read either. It's merely *different* reality, not *distant*. The Father, and Jesus, and the Holy Spirit, and the angels, and the twenty-four elders are all very, very close. It's just that right now we can't see them; we can't reach across and touch them yet. But the day will certainly come when we'll be surrounded by the overwhelming sound of trumpets and voices, and no one will ask, "Would you please turn the stero down?" The sounds will belong to the new heaven and the new earth, and so will we.

Revelation puts the fear of God into the heart of anyone who has spent some time with the Bible. Reading the Bible, studying it, trying to learn more about Jesus at its center is not a whimsical hobby for a few rare souls who happen to be interested in religious things. The Bible is the only link we have between where we are and where we're going. This gives it its shimmering glory and its fearsome intensity. As we close off our study of the Bible in the rarefied atmosphere of Revelation, we suddenly sense that this is where it's all going to end.

Coming close to God in His book places us in an uncomfortable position. We've now been confronted by His promises; we know their every syllable and nuance. God comes to us and says, "Believe in my Son, and you will be saved." It sounds so very simple, like a bank advertisement telling us to stash away some money every month. But it's not simple. Believing in Jesus means surrendering to Him, loving Him, obeying Him, confessing Him as Lord, turning one's life over to Him.

Walking into the grace of God is not like spending an afternoon at the beach or an evening at the movies. This is crisis. This is judgment. What am I going to do with this Savior? The promises of God demand an answer. I think of the people of Israel who had all the promises but chose to be disobedient in the desert. The serpents came, the ground split open, and they learned what it meant to be literally plagued by God.

In the eleventh chapter of Revelation we hear the trumpet and the voices, and we see the terrifying judgment that accompanies full exposure to the rule of Christ. We also discover an almost unbelievable, unexpressible jubilation. Judgment cuts two directions at once.

The scene of judgment teaches that human life is not a joke. It is not an absurdity. Every human being is so important that God takes each one seriously—so seriously, that one can't escape God's notice even by dying: The day will come when even the dead will be judged (cf. Rev. 11:18).

The judgment of God is frightening, and moving toward it is distressing—but think how horrible it would be if there were no judgment. That would mean there really is no meaning to human experience. If there were no ultimate judgment, then there would be no difference between a young mother's decision to abort or to go through with the birth of an unplanned child whose heart beats within her womb. There would be no difference between assassination and healing, between sloth and ambition, between a scream and an oratorio. If there were no right and wrong, if ultimately all human action were to escape God's attentive judgment, then it really would make no difference that unrighteousness and injustice fester within the world, that millions gorge themselves while billions starve.

But look: In Revelation there's the breathtaking announcement that the Lord's ultimate judgment is absolutely certain—THEREFORE, all human existence has meaning.

The book of Revelation assures us that God will one day collect all the tangled threads of human history, from the day Adam and Eve miserably mistook Satan's promises to the last day of time; He will bring them all together and weave one golden cord. And that is the great and only defense against cynicism and despair. I don't think I could stand the pressure of reality if I didn't have this book with Christ as its center and judgment at its end. If the mighty message of the twenty-four elders is not a fact, then rip off the paper, burn the book, bury this man, and stamp the earth hard across my grave. Samuel Beckett would be right: The only utterance worth making in such a universe would be one long, low, agonized "Aghhhhh . . .hhhHHghA!!"

But as the trumpets sound and voices in heaven rise to a crescendo, the message is clear! Christ is Lord. Those who reign with Christ are first united with Him through faith. What is that faith? It's not a vague, undefinable condition of one's soul; on the contrary, it's a believer's specific response to the Bible, God's very specific Word.

And we see again that the Bible is one book, like a finely woven cloth without a seam. When the door of the heavenly temple swings open, we see the cherubim wings spread over the ark of the covenant—or, as Today's English Version calls it, "The Covenant Box." We remember its construction; we see David dancing jubilantly as the box was brought into Jerusalem; we recall that it was once lost. This is the ark, this quaint box containing the covenant contract—God's commandments, Aaron's budding rod—symbolizing God's grace.

We remember that later there was another box—a feeding box in a Bethlehem stable. It, too, contained God's grace. By then it was no symbol. It was a person, Jesus.

And now we must respond to all of this. What is our response? Well, what's the appropriate response to a promise? Acceptance. Thanks. Faith. Faith is believing the promises of God, and that's the response for which He waits.

Christianity is simply promises, promises, promises. As the silence of the Bible gives way to the brilliant sound of the trumpet, as we hear the mighty heavenly voices and the twenty-four elders announcing Christ's eternal rule, we know that the promises can't be ignored. They insist that we respond.

*   *   *

> The promises of the Lord can be trusted; they are as genuine as silver refined seven times in the furnace.
>
> (Ps. 12:6, TEV)

Suggested Bible Readings

The One who was in the beginning is the One who stands gloriously revealed in the end. The Word has become the Lamb; and the Lamb is the mighty King. The voices of every creature in heaven and on earth proclaim His honor and glory.

Revelation 1-5; John 1:1-18

137